CYNDI

LAUPER

Also Published by Ballantine Books:

BOY GEORGE AND CULTURE CLUB

BRUCE SPRINGSTEEN

DURAN DURAN

EURYTHMICS

VAN HALEN

CYNDI LAUPER

K. K. Willis, Jr.

BALLANTINE BOOKS • NEW YORK

Copyright © 1984 by K. K. Willis, Jr.

All rights reserved under International and Pan-American Copyright Conventions. Published in the United States by Ballantine Books, a division of Random House, Inc., New York, and simultaneously in Canada by Random House of Canada Limited, Toronto.

Library of Congress Catalog Card Number: 84-91174
ISBN 0-345-32202-9

Manufactured in the United States of America

First Edition: October 1984
Cover photos by Ebet Roberts
Interior book design by Michaelis/Carpelis Design

CONTENTS

ACKNOWLEDGMENTS

Thanks to Nancy Schuman, Doug Bowes, Doug Fischer, Sue Barnett, Mark Friedman, Marvin & Gladys, Flip McCarthy, Eliot Wald, and Toni Zules for all-around research aid; Rhonda Markowitz of Polydor for steering me in the right direction; and Tessa Marquis for her encyclopedic knowledge of the record industry.

K. K. Willis, Jr.

CYNDI LAUPER

INTRODUCTION

*E*arly 1984: Across North America people discover that an outrageously dressed young woman by the name of Cyndi Lauper is in the process of taking over their television sets. The standard response to the first sighting of this strange invader is "Who is *that*?!" The invader's look is, to say the least, a novelty on prime-time TV. Her wild mane of hair glows in several shades of radioactive red. A close examination of her hairdo reveals a set of delicately shaved stripes or crisscrosses—that is, if her head isn't wrapped up in a gauzy Day-Glo bandanna. Her makeup... well, let's just say that it's likely to be anything from a laid-back eyeshadow job in molten gold to an asymmetric action painting that would look great on a new-wave Klingon princess. She's wearing a tight, colorful corset from the fifties, long, multihued crinolines, and bangles—some displaying peace signs— by the kilo. She's barefoot. Oddly enough, this psychedelic potpourri adds up to a unified whole: It's the costume of either a flamenco dancer–turned–urban guerrilla or a gypsy from outer space. And then she starts to sing. Her voice is amazing, an octave-vaulting instrument that soars for the rockers, sobs for the tear-jerkers, and has a built-in assortment of sound effects—harmonics, giggles, pops, squeaks, and yodels. She stops singing and says a few words into the microphone. Wonder of wonders: *She sounds like Betty Boop!*

Who *is* she?

"I first saw Cyndi on the New Show," says one recently converted Lauperite. "I'm always skeptical about new performers, especially if they dress funny. She came on the screen and I thought, 'Oh no.' Then she started to sing 'Girls Just Want to Have Fun,' which I'd never heard before. By the end of the first verse, I was thinking, 'Hmm, she's pretty good.' By the end of the second verse, I was saying, 'Hey, she's for real!' By the end of the song, I was on my way to the nearest all-night record store."

Thousands—millions—of others agreed. As her first album, *She's So Unusual*, and her first single, "Girls Just Want to Have Fun," were rocketing up the charts, petite (five-foot-three-inch) Cyndi Lauper (pronounced *lawper*, rhymes with *pauper*) was embarking on her campaign to take over the airwaves, appearing on network TV, on cable (the "Girls" video was getting heavy airplay on MTV), and on the radio. What's even more amazing is how quickly she became not only the hottest female vocalist in America but in Canada, England, Germany, France, Italy, Australia, Japan—all over the world! In a matter of months she'd come from nowhere to become a true international pop phenomenon.

But did she really come from nowhere? Is she a fluke, a girl just looking for fun, a flash in the pan who happened to get lucky? Or, like other overnight sensations, did Cyndi Lauper spend years in obscurity, toiling at her craft, preparing herself for the big time? And what is she really like, behind the flash, the wild clothes, the spacey makeup, the squawky cartoon-character voice? Where did she come from? Where is she going?

Who is she?

A KID FROM
THE BOROUGHS

*A*t first glance, Cyndi Lauper appears to be the wild girl lurking within every girl, the girl who not only wants to have fun but knows how to go out and *do it*. But it's soon apparent that there's more to Cyndi than fun. For one thing, she can sing. Boy, can she sing. Then there's her stage presence and not just when she's singing. It's there when she's presenting a Grammy with Rodney Dangerfield. Or clowning around with Johnny Carson on "The Tonight Show." Or talking to her audiences at a live performance.

Then there's the fact that she writes or cowrites many of her songs.

And that she is the driving artistic force behind her music videos.

That she plans to design her own line of clothing.

That she's considering writing a book one day.

Above all, that despite the Fun Girl image she is a serious artist at the core.

The time for Cyndi Lauper is now. With the release of *She's So Unusual*, her debut album on Portrait Records, this veteran New York rocker comes into her own with ten tracks of vibrant, heartfelt pop-rock. It's a sound that is firmly rooted in the best American musical traditions, but with an eye (and ear) for the technological advances of today....

From a Portrait Records press release

Female performers have always had a tough time making it in the male-dominated realm of rock 'n' roll. Only a handful of women have managed to stay at the top of the charts for any length of time. Many of those who reached the heights—from Connie Francis to Janis Joplin—had trouble staying there; a number of them lost their sense of direction and experienced tragic crash landings. Even today, when there are more female rock 'n' rollers than ever before, it's unusual to find one who is truly in charge of her own career.

Cyndi Lauper is an exception.

> My goal is to become not just a successful singer, but a complete artist. I've spent a long time working on my voice, just the way an athlete has to build up his body and keep in condition. I'd like to perfect my songwriting and develop my visual side with things like directing the album cover or planning the video. I want to be a great artist, to really say something, to be remembered.
>
> *From a Portrait Records press release*

By taking control of her own career, by insisting on her artistic integrity, Cyndi Lauper is breaking with a tradition that goes back to the roots of rock 'n' roll.

Back in the fifties, most rock stars, regardless of how much they knew about music, had very little knowledge of the workings of the music business. Consequently, they were like putty in the hands of their managers, publicists, and record companies. They were told what to sing, what to wear, how to pose for photographers, what to tell reporters. . . . in short, their job was to live up to the images manufactured by the people around them. Even the biggest stars were in this position. Elvis Presley, for example, in the early days, practically needed the permission of his manager, Colonel Tom Parker, to blow his nose.

Many a performer had more image than talent— there were plenty of star-for-a-day types who looked good but whose musical skills were nonexistent. Some promoters even specialized in finding good-looking teenagers, shoving them in front of a microphone (it didn't matter if they could sing), recording the results, and foisting on the world—at least for the next month or two—an instant teen idol.

In other words, the performers and the music they made were treated very much like any other kind of product, to be bought and sold and adjusted to meet prevailing market conditions. Cyndi Lauper might have had a lot of trouble getting a producer to listen to her if she'd come along in the late fifties—performers weren't supposed to know what they were doing back then.

Fortunately, the situation began to loosen up in the 1960s. Musicians like the Beatles and Bob Dylan broke the pattern by writing and performing their own material, saying what they wanted to say, making their own career moves with minimal managerial interference. Rock 'n' roll may not have grown up, but it had at least reached adolescence; musicians were now able to conduct themselves as artists, making their own choices and living with the consequences. (This isn't to say that rock 'n' roll "packaging" was a lost art. The most extreme example from the mid sixties is probably that of the Monkees, who were an image before they were a band. The producers first came up with the idea, then auditioned hundreds of musicians and actors until they had a group that looked right. In some quarters—we're not about to say which—the practice continues to this day!) More recently, according to Cyndi, none other than Michael Jackson helped to loosen up the industry for her kind of music. "The industry was very tight," Cyndi told Marianne Meyer of *Interview* magazine. "I guess we have to thank Michael Jackson for reviving it. God bless the dear boy, he made room for people like me."

By the time the '80s rolled around, the world and the music business was finally ready for Cyndi Lauper.

Cyndi Lauper's story begins in the New York City boroughs of Brooklyn and Queens.

When people from around the world think of New York City, they're likely to conjure up images of glittering skyscrapers, sophisticated nightclubs, expensive restaurants, Broadway openings—in short, the flashy side of the Big Apple. Those who live in the City know that while this image may fit the island of Manhattan, it surely does not apply to the other boroughs: the Bronx, Brooklyn, Queens, and Staten Island. Manhattanites, consequently, tend to be condescending toward their cousins in the boroughs, referring to those who have the nerve to commute regularly into Manhattan as bridge and tunnel people. To accuse someone of speaking with a Queens or Brooklyn accent is, for a Manhattanite, the ultimate put-down.

It isn't that the boroughs lack sophistication. Each can hold its own, culturally, with most other North American cities. The problem, the reason people tend to look down at the boroughs, is their *context*. All but a handful of cities in the world seem provincial when compared with Manhattan, but the comparison is usually irrelevant. If you lived in Detroit or Denver or Dallas or D.C., why would you waste your time constantly comparing your city with the Big Apple? If you live in the boroughs, however, the comparison is inevitable. It is nearly impossible to travel west on, say, Queens Boulevard, surrounded by fast-food establishments and nondescript low-rise apartment buildings, without noticing the gleaming spires of Manhattan in the distance, without wondering: "Why am I *here* and not *there*?"

Manhattan may be only a half hour away, but that half hour can seem like a lifetime.

It's probably more difficult for a talented young person from Queens or Brooklyn to get up the courage to move to Manhattan, to have a shot at the big time, than it is for someone from just about anywhere else.

If you're from Detroit, Denver, Dallas, or D.C., you're free to imagine yourself taking the Big Apple by storm. If you're from the boroughs, though, you might be a little less sure of yourself. Growing up in the shadow of Manhattan can induce feelings of inferiority that can cause you to abandon your dreams at an early age.

Cyndi Lauper was one talented kid from the boroughs who, despite many opportunities to lose faith in herself, never abandoned her dreams.

> ... Her story began in Brooklyn, New York, where Cyndi was "almost born in a taxicab, on the way to Boulevard Hospital in Queens." ...
>
> *From a Portrait Records press release*

Cynthia Lauper's family lived in Williamsburg, Brookyn. The famous taxi ride, according to the press release, may account for her "lifelong infatuation with Hollywood and all its glorious dramatic cliches." Cyndi is mum about the date of her natal taxi ride ("I'm not a car—it doesn't matter"), but according to an old band blurb it seems to have happened on the 20th of June, 1953.

Today, Williamsburg, Brookyn, is a tense, rundown neighborhood populated mainly by blacks and Hasidic Jews who are frequently at war with each other. The Williamsburg of the early 1950s contained a different ethnic mix but was still a very rough place to bring up a family.

It hadn't always been that way. Back in the 1800s, many of the citizens of northwest Brooklyn were farmers who shipped their produce to the big city—Manhattan—on a ferry that left from Williamsburg. The area grew as a number of distilleries and breweries—attracted by the proximity to the city, to raw materials, and to labor—were established there. Later, it flourished as a fashionable resort, complete with hotels patronized by the likes of Jim Fisk, William C. Whitney, and Commodore Vanderbilt. It's hard to picture it—

especially if you've seen Williamsburg lately—but for
many wealthy New Yorkers, "going to the country"
meant taking a pleasant boat ride across the East River
to Brooklyn.

Then, in 1903, the Williamsburg Bridge was completed, and as the rich folk might have said, "There
goes the neighborhood!" Almost overnight the com-
munity was transformed into an immigrant district as
the overflow from Manhattan's Lower East Side spilled
across the bridge. The wealthy families cleared out;
their elegant mansions and large brownstone homes
were hastily divided into multiple-occupancy dwellings
that would house the newcomers who arrived in wave
after wave for the next fifty or sixty years.

Cut to 1953 and the Williamsburg into which Cyndi
Lauper was born. Long gone and forgotten was the
vacation paradise for New York's leading families. Instead there were endless streets of ugly tenement buildings, punctuated by the odd, rubbish-strewn vacant lot
and an occasional stretch of shabby one- or two-family
homes, surrounding the dilapidated old brownstones
and mansions. In the eternal rumbling twilight beneath
the trestles of the elevated subway, teenaged members of various ethnic groups fought each other with
baseball bats, switchblades, and other indigenous
American weapons.

Cyndi's mother (who is Italian) and her father were
struggling, like most people in Williamsburg. (Cyndi
says her family was "not rich, but not exactly poor
either.") Her father worked hard to make ends meet
while her mother did her best to raise three children—
Cyndi, her kid brother, Butch, and her older sister,
Ellen. When Cyndi was five years old, her mother and
father were divorced.

We're talking about a girl who had every reason *not*
to be having a whole lot of fun.

After the divorce, Cyndi's mother and the three
kids moved across the Queens border to Ozone Park,
a working-class neighborhood that is the home of

Aqueduct Racetrack, located a stone's throw from Idlewild, or, as it is now called, John F. Kennedy International Airport. Ozone Park was still a long way from Broadway, but the sidewalks were a little cleaner, the buildings were not so run-down, the streets were safer at night: It was a definite improvement over Williamsburg.

Young Cyndi, though, was still out in the ozone. She didn't feel that she belonged—she was becoming a genuine misfit, an outcast who kept pretty much to herself. Even as a child, she was regarded as "so unusual." "People always have looked at me in a funny way," Cyndi told *Record* magazine. "I was always out of place. Out of place and out of time. Out of step with everyone else. It drove me crazy. I didn't know what was wrong with me or why I was so different. Nobody loved me. Nobody liked me. And I'm so *weird*. And I'm a *geek*. And *why* am I so weird?" This was the late fifties, remember, when "unusual" wasn't such a great thing to be. Her mother grew so concerned that she took to lighting candles to Saint Jude, the patron saint of desperate cases. What may have prevented Cyndi from growing up to be an adult outcast or a full-fledged nerd (even though she insists that she is now and always has been a nerd) was that her mother actively encouraged her creativity. Today Cyndi considers this to have been her "saving grace."

It strains the imagination, considering the spectacular performer (and wild dresser) she later became, but Cyndi was once a parochial-school girl, attending a Catholic school not far from where she lived. It didn't last long—she was given the boot, apparently because it was a no-no to have a divorced mother. After that she was sent to another Catholic institution, this one a convent boarding school upstate. Cyndi hated it. Even now she refers to it as a torture chamber, remembering how the nuns seemed to enjoy dishing out corporal punishment to the innocent young girls who had the misfortune to be imprisoned there. "I had my knuckles smacked," Cyndi says, "I had my hair pulled, I had my face scrubbed with soap and I had to wash my face with Noxema because my face breaks out from soap, and I was told how vain I was."

That experience left her with a clean face but may have made a permanent mark on Cyndi's psyche. "I'm a traumatized person," she told *Rock Video* magazine. "I was traumatized as a child, and after you've gone through trauma, you expect more trauma. You don't expect good things, you expect more bad things, because bad things have happened." She became convinced that all big institutions—especially church and state—are oppressors of women. (In later years she was to reach a similar conclusion about certain segments of the music business.) After six months in the convent school she focused her creative energies on getting out. Of course, she succeeded.

Back in Ozone Park she still looked different from the other kids. "No matter how hard I tried to look normal, there was always something that wasn't right," she says. "I'd put on false eyelashes, and one would always curl up." By the time she was twelve she was dying her hair garish colors and wearing outrageous makeup and clothes in an effort to change her life and become somebody—*anybody*—else. It was a conscious decision to indulge her individuality, to ignore the kids and teachers who criticized her for being different, to recognize and, if possible, avoid the institutions of oppression. There were still problems, of course. School, even public school with no nuns to push her around, just didn't seem to be the place for Cyndi—even if she did occasionally have fun entertaining her classmates in the school yard with a song or her locally famous Al Jolson impersonation.

Cyndi has been known to claim that she was born singing. Actually, she started singing publicly when she was only five: Dressed in shorts, a shirt, and sneakers, her hair cropped short, she'd perform Broadway show tunes for the old ladies in the neighborhood, who would give her quarters and send her back to her mom. Their favorites were Cyndi's renditions of "Bali Ha'i" and "Happy Talk" from Rodgers and Hammerstein's *South Pacific*.

Like most kids, the first music she heard was whatever was playing around the house. Her mom's tastes were eclectic—everything from the operatic Eileen Farrell and Mario Lanza to Fanny Brice, the Boswell Sisters, Barbra Streisand, Steve Lawrence and Eydie Gorme, to Broadway musicals, to Ella Fitzgerald, Louis Armstrong, and Billie Holiday, even to Ethel Merman! ("I really loved her," Cyndi says of Merman. "That woman had something really special.") According to her mother, "She mimicked them all."

"It's a funny thing," says Cyndi. "The human voice is a great healer, and it always made me feel better when I sang. If I was sad, I would sing."

Cyndi's mother's tastes may have been eclectic but not eclectic enough to encompass rock 'n' roll, which was to be her daughter's true calling. We can assume that Cyndi and her siblings discovered *that* kind of music without any parental assistance. (Cyndi's mom may have helped a little—she occasionally drove her kids into Greenwich Village to look at the beatniks. "Wow," the kids would say, "look at that guy. He's got long hair and everything. He's got a guitar!" Cyndi now thinks her mother was as fascinated with the scene as her kids were.)

In those days, AM radio in the New York area was full of good rock 'n' roll stations—WMCA, WABC, WINS, WMGM, and many smaller ones that came and went: It was rock 'n' roll–radio paradise. With a spin of the dial you could tune in a song by Elvis Presley, Buddy Holly and the Crickets, Jackie Wilson, Frankie Lymon and the Teenagers, the Everly Brothers, Smokey Robinson and the Miracles, the Drifters, or the great "girl groups" like the Ronettes, Little Eva, the Supremes, the Marvelettes, the Shirelles, the Chantels, Claudine Clark, the Chiffons, the

Crystals. . . . the list was endless. And Cyndi, who had little else going for her at the time, must have heard them all.

INFLUENCES

Cyndi grew up in a house where there was always music playing. The following list includes some of Cyndi's mother's favorite recording artists from that period, artists Cyndi says she heard and enjoyed as a child and who have had a lasting influence on her music. Some of them may seem to be unlikely influences, but who are we to argue?

EILEEN FARRELL, a well-known and highly respected dramatic soprano, was one of Cyndi's mom's favorite singers. Farrell performed in concert and made records from 1940 on, making her debut at the Metropolitan Opera in 1960 in the title role of Gluck's *Alceste*. Later in her career she reached new fans with a number of jazzy recordings of pop tunes.

MARIO LANZA was a tenor with what has been described as a phenomenal instrument. He performed both opera and popular music. Many regarded him as the successor to Caruso. During the last ten years of his short, undisciplined life he also appeared in a number of motion picture musicals, including *That Midnight Kiss*, *Seven Hills of Rome*, and *The Great Caruso*.

FANNY BRICE was a singer and vaudeville entertainer. While she appeared in a number of movies (including *My Man* in 1928 and *Ziegfeld Follies* in 1945) and made records, many people today know her through the movies made *about* her, especially the two Barbra Streisand vehicles, *Funny Girl* and *Funny Lady*.

ETHEL MERMAN is probably the entertainer least likely to be chosen as an influence on Cyndi Lauper or, for that matter, on any other rock 'n' roller. However, Cyndi insists she's a die-hard Merman fan. Merman, who belted songs with a voice that could be heard for miles, appeared on Broadway, in movies (including a cameo in the original *Airplane*), and on TV.

LOUIS "SATCHMO" ARMSTRONG, the great jazz trumpet virtuoso, became known for his unique, mouth-full-of-marbles singing style late in his career. His record of "Hello Dolly!" sold over a million discs, which in itself may be considered inspiring.

BILLIE HOLIDAY was the torch singer's torch singer. "God Bless the Child," "My Man," "Mean to Me," "Ain't Nobody's Business (If I Do)," and many of her other performances are classics. Cyndi says that when she was studying jazz she learned to phrase by listening to Billie Holiday and Lester Young.

LESTER YOUNG was a tenor saxophonist who played with the bands of Count Basie and Fletcher Henderson, among others; he also recorded with Billie Holiday.

THE BOSWELL SISTERS, Connee, Martha, and Vet, sang with big bands, on Broadway, and in a number of films during the thirties and forties.

ELLA FITZGERALD is still a sensational singer with a vocal range of several octaves. Her ability to change her voice's colorings at will may have inspired Cyndi to figure out how to do it, too.

STEVE LAWRENCE AND EYDIE GORME: Do you remember Eydie's "Blame it on the Bossa Nova"? Hmm...didn't think so.

BARBRA STREISAND: Owner of another great vocal instrument. A late arrival on Cyndi's mother's list—she appeared on the scene in the early sixties, was an immediate hit on television, and went on to have a stellar recording and motion picture career.

RICHARD RODGERS and OSCAR HAMMERSTEIN were not singers but composers of Broadway musicals; many consider them to be the greatest ever. Their work includes *Oklahoma!*, *Carousel*, *The King and I*, *Flower Drum Song*, *The Sound of Music*, and Cyndi's favorite, *South Pacific*.

With Cyndi, as with so many others, the big musical breakthrough came when the British Invasion first hit the American airwaves. It's hard to believe now, but in 1964 people listening for the first time to the Beatles doing "I Want to Hold Your Hand" were astonished—the harmonies of John Lennon and Paul McCartney were like nothing they'd ever heard before. Cyndi was particularly fascinated by Lennon's mysterious lower harmony. She and her sister, Ellen, would sing Beatles songs together, often while they did the dishes, with Cyndi on low harmony.

"Those guys," she says of the Beatles, "were a great inspiration because they came from poor beginnings. I always thought from reading their stories that there was a chance for me." She never managed to sound anything like a Beatle, though, which was so frustrating that she temporarily gave up singing. It would be interesting to see Cyndi perform some of those early Beatles tunes today, wouldn't it?

Well before the advent of the British Invasion, there began to stir another pop movement that would catch Cyndi's attention: folk music. Folk music, by definition, had been around for years; along with the blues (which in itself may be considered a form of folk music), it was an important precursor of rock 'n' roll. In the late fifties and early sixties, though, there was a folk explosion. Suddenly folk music, or a commercial version of it, could be heard on the radio back-to-back with Elvis and Buddy Holly. At first only the likes of the Kingston Trio, with their slick harmonies, slick production, and slick crewcuts, received any attention, but soon such "true" folkies as Peter, Paul, and Mary (slick in their own right), Joan Baez, Odetta, the Weavers, and Bob Dylan began to attract an audience. In addition to its simple, moving songs that appealed to both the emotions and the intellect, folk music seemed a lot easier to play than rock 'n' roll: All you needed was a guitar, a few chords, maybe a harmonica; a great voice, as Dylan proved, was optional.

But what most excited Cyndi about the new generation of folk singers—and rockers as well—was that they were beginning to write their own songs. On hearing Joni Mitchell for the first time, Cyndi says, "It inspired me to do something, to feel like there was a place for me." And, when she heard Grace Slick of the Jefferson Airplane, "I couldn't believe it. I thought that was fabulous."

Cyndi's "retirement" from singing didn't last long. She soon discovered her sister's guitar, taught herself to strum a few chords, and—along with thousands of her peers—became an urban folkie. She played in parks around town and at the occasional hootenanny and started writing her own songs. She was also politically active, taking part in a number of peace marches opposing the war in Vietnam.

Although Cyndi was beginning to get her musical act together, the rest of her life was still a mess. She was doing poorly in school and had begun to doubt her own intelligence. "Creative kids," Cyndi says, "are often mistaken for stupid kids, and I was mistakenly taken for stupid. *I* even thought I was stupid." All told, she attended a total of four high schools, finally receiving her General Equivalency Diploma directly from New York State. Her mother—whose second marriage had ended in a second divorce—was working long days as a waitress to support the family. Ozone Park was beginning to drive Cyndi crazy. Everywhere she looked she saw women as losers: Her mother wasting her life waiting on tables, other women turning old before their time from the slavery of supporting their families and raising a bunch of kids. Realizing that the only way for her to be happy was to get out of there, she packed her bags and—at the age of seventeen—left town.

INFLUENCES

When Cyndi was old enough to choose her own music, she chose to listen to rock 'n' roll and folk music. Here are some of the artists who have influenced her over the years:

THE BEATLES: John Lennon, Paul McCartney, George Harrison, and Ringo Star, the four mopheads from Liverpool, spearheaded the British Invasion of 1964. With their mysterious harmonies, their driving beat, and their ingenious and prolific songwriting, they inspired Cyndi and an entire generation of young American protorockers.

GRACE SLICK: It depressed Cyndi to realize that no matter how hard she tried, she'd never be able to sound like the Beatles. Then the Jefferson Airplane's *Surrealistic Pillow* album (with the songs "Somebody to Love," "White Rabbit," et al.) came out in 1967, and Cyndi discovered in singer Grace Slick a role model for a *female* rocker.

JONI MITCHELL, who came along about a year after the Airplane, also impressed Cyndi as a woman who was making her own music. Not only did she write, sing, and play her own songs, she also painted her own album covers. Joni Mitchell, Cyndi says, "inspired me to do something, feel like there was a place for me."

ELVIS PRESLEY: If the responsibility for rock 'n' roll can be pinned on any single individual whose name is not Little Richard or Chuck Berry, that individual would have to be Elvis. Cyndi's an Elvis fan from way back. As Buddy Holly said, "Without Elvis, none of us could have made it." And speaking of Buddy Holly...

BUDDY HOLLY, who died in a 1959 airplane crash at the age of twenty-two, was a rock original. His highly mannered vocal style was full of hiccups, baby talk, squeals, squeaks, pops, stutters, and, in the words of Jonathan Cott, "sudden glides from deep bass to falsetto (and back again), revealing the child inside the man, the man inside the child." Listening to Cyndi, on "She Bop," for example, you can't help but be aware of the Buddy Holly influence.

EDDIE COCHRAN, another fifties rocker to die at the age of twenty-two (in a London car accident), wrote and recorded the classic "Summertime Blues," later covered by the Who and others. An American rockabilly singer in the Elvis Presley mold, Cochran was one of Cyndi's—and Blue Angel's—inspirations.

CARL PERKINS: "Well it's one for the money, two for the show, three to get ready, now go cat go..." So begins "Blue Suede Shoes," the rock classic written and first performed by Carl Perkins. Elvis may have made it a hit by covering it in 1956, but it was Carl's song. So were "Matchbox," "Everybody's Trying to Be My Baby," and "Honey Don't," all covered by the Beatles (and sung by Ringo!). Carl Perkins is still a rockabilly giant.

FRANKIE LYMON was the lead singer of the Teenagers and cowriter of their huge hit, "Why Do Fools Fall in Love?" Until his voice changed, Lymon was the premier boy soprano of his day and one of the undisputed stars of doo-wop.

CYNDI
ON HER OWN

$\mathcal{S}$ome teenagers run away from home because they don't get along with their parents. Cyndi left for other reasons. Sure, she and her mother had had their disagreements, but the main reason she left was not to flee her family but to get away from Queens, to be on her own in the world, to try to find herself. It might have been the folk-music influence—there are hundreds of folk songs about hoppin' freight trains, goin' who-knows-where, leavin' friends and family behind. Or maybe Cyndi was driven by a force—call it fate—to wander aimlessly for a while, gathering experience that she would draw upon later. In any case, it was time to move on. Cyndi hit the road with her faithful mutt, Sparkle (the same dog who now makes guest appearances in her videos), by her side.

At first she stayed with a friend on Long Island. Then it was time to move again. She traveled to Vermont, where she enrolled in an art college not far from Stowe. To pay for room and board for herself and Sparkle, she took odd jobs—waiting on tables, working as a model in painting classes, whatever came along. As usual, Cyndi was unhappy in school; she was beginning to identify with another outcast, her favorite artist, Vincent van Gogh. To add to her problems, she wound up living with a young man who, it turned out, was prone to domestic violence. Cyndi finally said,

"Whoa, this is not for me. I don't have to live like this," and packed her bags.

She and Sparkle headed for the Great White North: Canada. They wound up in the woods north of Toronto, living in a tent, getting close to nature. For a couple of weeks everything was fine—Cyndi spent her time sketching while Sparkle chased the local fauna. Soon, though, Cyndi, ever the city girl, had had enough of trees—she was homesick. It was time to fold up the tent and head south again.

Cyndi was approaching the bottom. After nearly a year on the road, she found herself back in Ozone Park feeling as if she'd accomplished nothing. Was she destined to spend her days chained to a kitchen stove, tending a bunch of screaming kids like the other women around her? While the odd jobs she continued taking seemed to argue against this possibility—she pierced ears, worked as a secretary, sold karate and judo lessons, sold stockings in a shoe store, and even worked as a hot walker (the person who walks a horse after it runs) at a nearby racetrack—she was still worried that she'd be stuck in Ozone Park forever. To make matters worse, she was feeling like even more of an outcast than ever before. Because of the way she dressed, Cyndi says that "people threw rocks at me." "Sometimes," she told *Rolling Stone* recently, "I felt so *crumbled*."

She could have given up her dreams there and then, but as low as she felt, she refused to admit defeat. There was something burning inside of her, a creative force just waiting to burst out. If only she had an outlet for her creativity . . .

Then it came to her. There was one thing she knew she could do as well as anyone else: *sing*.

Why did it take her so long to realize this? "Because," she says, "every time I tried to sing, people would say, 'Oh, Cyndi, don't sing, you don't sing that good.' Or I'd sing a lot, and they'd say, 'Please, Cyndi, please, I can't take it anymore.' Or I would play my guitar and sing when I was inspired, which was always around twelve o'clock at night, when nobody else wanted to hear it."

Shaking off the criticism, she focused her energies and started singing seriously. At first she sang on street corners in Greenwich Village, living for a while in a bus parked on Third Street. (This was at a time when there were quite a few young people living in odd domiciles around the Village and the East Village.) "I was lucky," she says. "I did so many crazy things, and nothing ever happened to me." Finally, in 1974, she got her first job as a professional musician. The band was called Doc West, and it played the Long Island bar circuit. It was a long way from the big time, but never mind—at least Cyndi was being paid to make music. Disco was at its height in the mid-seventies, and Doc West played cover versions of all the big disco hits. Cyndi was primarily a backup singer with the band, although she did get to sing lead on a few Patti LaBelle and Chaka Khan numbers. She also performed a decidedly nondisco medley of songs by the late Janis Joplin.

CYNDI ON HER "MOST PRECIOUS GIFT"

"My voice is my most precious gift. It's hard to explain—it's almost like it's got a persona of its own, and I cherish it very much."

As exciting as it was to be singing in a band, it didn't take long for the novelty to wear off. "In bands like that," Cyndi told *New York* magazine, "there's a certain boys'-club atmosphere, and a girl will have a difficult time. I took a lot of abuse. And then we were always working to make a truck payment, or to buy equipment that would be outdated as soon as you turned around. . . ."

Cyndi, a rock 'n' roller to the core, had another problem with Doc West: She was not what you'd call a big discomaniac. In fact, performing disco tunes night after night was becoming a drag. As if that weren't bad enough, her Joplin act was getting out of control—not only was she beginning to feel haunted by Janis's spirit, but the people around her were starting to mention that Cyndi's singing was sounding exactly like Joplin's. Add to this the fact that Doc West made Cyndi perform in funny clothes (well, they were probably normal at the time—which means they were funny from her point of view!), and you'll understand why she soon had to quit the band.

Cyndi didn't look back. In no time she had put together Flyer, another Long Island bar band. The good news was that Flyer played rock 'n' roll music, which was a big improvement for Cyndi. (Disco was still big, of course, but it was beginning to experience a rock 'n' roll backlash—Disco Sucks buttons had become a de rigueur fashion accessory for true rockers; rock radio stations from Massachusetts to California were sponsoring disco record–smashing contests in parking lots and shopping malls.) The bad news was that, like Doc West, Flyer was primarily a cover band that played other people's songs.

Why did Cyndi—who we now know is perfectly capable of writing dynamite original material—need to work in cover bands? For one thing, it was a matter of circumstance. Playing, say, at My Father's Place, a popular club in Roslyn, Long Island, isn't very different from playing bars in any number of other suburbs across the country: The band's job is to entertain by sounding familiar, to play songs that the audience already knows, and to play them the way the original artists did, lick for lick, line for line. Creativity, inventiveness, and originality may work in the big city (if you're good enough to pull it off), but a bar band in the 'burbs must conform or be fired. Remember, too, that while Cyndi was bursting with talent, she didn't yet have the wherewithal and confidence to strike off on her own—after all, she'd been performing professionally for only a short while.

Cyndi and the other members of Flyer worked hard, practicing days and playing nights. Cyndi's voice was improving with each passing week, and her self-confidence was growing—she was quickly developing into the dynamic vocalist and unrestrained performer she is today. Unfortunately, Flyer's audiences didn't fully appreciate what they were seeing and hearing. Night after night Cyndi was on stage belting out rock 'n' roll classics to people who sat there sipping drinks, talking to each other, and complaining that the songs didn't sound exactly like the originals. They also complained that the crazy singer, Cyndi Whatever-her-name-is, didn't look like the typical female rock 'n' roller. "Hey," we can imagine someone saying, "I came here to see this band act like the Stones or Rod Stewart or the Jefferson Airplane. Why is she jumping around like that? Why is she wearing those funny clothes? Who *is* she?"

Of course, they had no way of knowing that for Cyndi it wasn't just a question of style. Having suffered the traumas of her childhood, she was actively trying to break the circle of suffering, to substitute a happy present for an unhappy past. One of the ways she does this is to wear clothes and jewelry that make her happy—and typical rock 'n' roll togs just don't do it for her. "I like to wear a lot of jewelry," she says, "because I like to look at it. It's just like perfume. You know why I wear perfume? So *I* can smell it. And I only wear what I like to smell. And I only color my hair the way I like to see it. And the same with my face and my clothes and my shoes. I like to wear neat shoes so when I'm walking and I look down at my feet, I can smile." Presumably, performing makes her so happy that she usually goes shoeless onstage.

And then, of course, there was the problem of her speaking voice. It's not that people on Long Island weren't accustomed to hearing a Queens accent. The native speech of Long Islanders is in fact closely related to "Noo Yawk" speech patterns. No, what was unusual about Cyndi Lauper was the high register of her speaking voice—especially when she was nervous or hassled—coupled with the exaggerated *intensity* of her Queens accent. (Bernadette Peters, by the way, is another star with a speaking voice near the upper end of the audible range. Do you know where she grew up? You got it: Ozone Park, Queens! One day scientists may discover that the air of Ozone Park contains a secret ingredient—could it be ozone? helium?—that causes certain talented individuals to develop cartoon-character voices.)

Cyndi herself describes her speaking voice as "ridiculous," but nowadays she has a sense of humor about it. When she was in Flyer, though, it wasn't so funny. It seemed that people in the audience were criticizing her simply because she was *different*, because she was so unusual. The sad part was that they weren't paying much attention to her singing, which was supposedly why they were there in the first place. The lack of acceptance was reminiscent of how things were back in the bad old school days; she found herself once again personally criticized and artistically thwarted.

Considering how hard she was working, she wasn't having very much fun.

"I cried my eyes out every night," she told *Record* magazine. "I liked to play in front of the people and sing to them, but a lot of the time they didn't know what the hell I was doing up there. Or even care. I got fired from gigs because I drew people away from the bar. And I was 'too small.' And 'only women with big tits can sing'—oh, *that* was one that killed me. The bad thing about those clubs is the managers and owners. They play with your head so that you don't know whether you're coming or going. I guess I still have anger toward those people."

Cyndi stuck it out with Flyer, even though she had to do things that weren't at all her style. But the endless playing in bars across Long Island finally took its toll. By 1977 she was exhausted.

The worst news, though, was that after three years of abuse Cyndi's vocal cords were completely shot.

GETTING INTO
SHAPE

*F*ortunately, Cyndi had enough sense to seek professional help for her voice. First she consulted a number of doctors. Their prognoses were unanimous: The patient was too far gone ever to sing again. Refusing to give up, Cyndi looked for another kind of help. Her friend Ellen Shaw, a singer, recommended that she speak with Katie Agresta, an opera singer and voice coach *extraordinaire*.

From the description of Katie Agresta that accompanies "Vocal Insights," the monthly column she writes for *The Music Paper*, a magazine for musicians:

> Katherine Agresta is a voice teacher and vocal therapist who currently resides in New York City where she runs a private practice. She has trained for seventeen years under the guidance of Dr. Edward J. Dwyer, who is a professor on the Doctoral Staff at Teachers College at Columbia University. Ms. Agresta has her Bachelor of Arts in Music from Hofstra University and is a native of Long Island, where she taught for several years before moving her practice to N.Y.C. Ms. Agresta has specialized in the teaching of rock singers and teaches them almost exclusively. She has taught guitar and piano and holds a N.Y. State Teaching Certificate for Adult Education Classes in Guitar. She has also taught music to every grade from third through high school.

Ms. Agresta also works as a recording consultant in N.Y.C. and is herself a professional singer.

Cyndi arrived at the door of Katie Agresta's cozy Manhattan studio in the spring of 1977. Her plan was to find a quick fix for her voice so she could get back to work. That wasn't the way it worked out, though. "She was in an emergency state," Agresta says, explaining that her definition of an emergency state for singers is when they have to sing and their voices simply won't work. There are a number of potential causes—nodules, polyps, laryngitis, vocal strain, and even an operation that hasn't healed properly.

Cyndi could not speak when she came to Agresta. Agresta recognized the symptoms—she was already the coach of many of the singers who worked the Long Island–New Jersey–Connecticut club circuit. Although Cyndi's intention was to stay with Flyer, she soon was convinced that that was impossible: Her voice just couldn't take it.

Realizing that the time had come to make some changes, Cyndi left Flyer—her friend Ellen Shaw replaced her—and started studying with her new voice coach. It was a good thing Cyndi quit the band when she did—she had the worst case of vocal burnout Agresta had seen up to that time; singers who continue to sing in that state face the possibility of wrecking their voices and never being able to sing again. Agresta explains that it's not uncommon to find cover-band singers in such dire straits because there's far more pushing and straining involved than in ordinary singing; they tend not to "sing their own voices" because they're so busy imitating everyone else. Plus, they usually don't have effective vocal techniques.

To better understand Cyndi—and how serious she is about singing—it helps to know something about the way Katie Agresta works.

Agresta was trained as an opera singer, but as there are very few positions available for professional opera singers, she had decided not long before she met Cyndi that she could support herself by applying her extensive knowledge of the human voice to rock singers. Why rock singers? First, her brother had been in a rock 'n' roll band for years—she'd spent lots of time around rock singers and knew the particular problems they faced:

"Opera singers have to be like bulls," she says, "'cause you're going to get up for three hours a night and sing over a sixty-piece orchestra: *you*, no microphone, no monitors, no help from anybody. The rock singer on the other hand is under that kind of pressure and more in many ways. They need the same kind of training, the same kind of stamina. They're performing under hot lights in very negative, smoky, adverse conditions. In the beginning of their careers, they very often will work in club bands. In the club bands they're working five and six nights a week, four and five sets a night, forty-five to fifty minutes a set with twenty minutes off. . . . you work from nine or ten at night to two or three in the morning, in the most horrible conditions—the dressing rooms are very often freezing cold, you know—so it's very bad for them."

Her second reason for working with rock singers? Quite simply, she isn't interested in coaching other opera singers. "Rock singers only," she laughs. "I won't teach my competition—that would be depressing."

How does a singer train?

There are three elements to Agresta's technique. First come the vocal exercises, which Agresta refers to as the "biofeedback" part because they help students learn to "communicate" with the many muscles associated with singing.

Second is nutrition. As Agresta says, "The singer has to be in perfect health. Here there's no difference from one singer to another. I don't care what style of music you do. A singer has to be perfectly healthy. Everything, *everything*, that affects you affects your voice. If you're a pianist and you get sick, the piano's fine and you're sick. If you're a singer and you're sick, you're sick and so is your instrument."

Third is exercise. If you are a singer, Agresta insists, "you're an athlete. You have to work out. When you run, you warm up, you stretch. For singing you stretch your singer's stretch. Singing training is very much athletic training because it's muscles and muscle co-ordination. For the singer it's very mysterious because it happens to be something that you train but you cannot see. You can only hear it. You go to sing: Laaa! And it comes out or it doesn't, and you don't know why."

Needless to say, very few rock singers ever attempt to solve the mystery by taking voice lessons. "Most people," laments Agresta, "maybe warm up, then perform. . . . they don't even think of warming *down*. Instead, they'll go out and have a beer after performing or smoke a joint. You know rock singers," she smiles. "Who knows what they'll do with themselves: smash a few guitars . . . What I try to do is to reeducate them and give them a system to go by, a way of living as a singer."

The archetypal rock 'n' roll lifestyle is, according to Agresta, a fast way to destroy your voice. "Some singers drink and sing, and they do great because they're so strong that the alcohol doesn't hurt them," she says. "That's not the case always. And it depends what they drink and how much they drink. Some people can have a beer and sing fabulously, have three and four beers. It doesn't bother them. Other people have one beer and it screws them up." The big problem with alcoholic beverages, she says, particularly gin and vodka, is that they dry out the throat and larynx, the focal point of the singer's instrument. What about smoking? "Horrible! And pot smoking is the worst. Cocaine is second in line—it numbs and then drips and then makes the larynx swollen. There are singers who've lost their voices because of coke. The people who are really,

really successful," she adds, "do not do drugs. They *can't*."

Cyndi corroborates this view of drugs in an interview she gave to Harold DeMuir in *The Aquarian*: "...I *did* do drugs when I was a teenager. When I was a young teenager, I saw my best friends drop dead. So when I see *adults* doing that...I can see how you might turn to that because you work so hard and you can't get to sleep when you have to sleep, and you can't get up when you have to get up. But there are ways to take care of yourself and do things naturally to unwind. When I see people on drugs I just think, 'Gee, that person isn't really in control of their faculties.'"

Just as meeting Katie Agresta proved to be a turning point for Cyndi, so was meeting Cyndi a turning point for Agresta. While Cyndi's voice was in the worst shape of any she'd worked with until then, since meeting Cyndi she's taken on equally difficult cases. "I took her case and ran with it," she says of Cyndi, "and then started specializing in that"—meaning tough cases—"because at that time heavy metal was big. I had people that, you know, I don't know how the hell they sang every night. Dee Snyder, the lead singer of Twisted Sister, is a perfect example. He's been my student for five years. We worked all that time to get him so that he could go out and scream every night and not lose his voice."

With her successful students spreading the word, new students have been flocking to Agresta's studio. She now has two teachers assisting her; altogether they have close to a hundred students. In order to reach an even wider audience, she is now planning a book to explain her technique. If all goes well, Katie Agresta foresees the day when she'll be opening her own school for rock singers.

Despite the number of people who have come to Katie Agresta for help, taking voice lessons is not stan-

dard procedure for rock singers. One reason many of
them resist vocal training is that they feel it would ruin
their characteristic style or, worse, make them sound
like opera singers. At this, Agresta can only smile.
"What they don't realize," she explains, "is that even
if they trained for fifteen years, they still would have
to do a whole bunch of very specific things to acquire
the opera sound. There's no way they're going to sing
like an opera singer." She should know—she's been
in opera training herself for twenty-one years!

Although Cyndi was so hoarse she could hardly talk
when they first met, Agresta immediately realized she
had the makings of a star: "I could tell she was great,
even before I heard her sing." How did she know? "I
just knew. I don't know how I knew, but I just knew.
The logistics of what happened are that I had told her,
'Bring a tape of yourself so I can hear what your voice
sounded like before you got to this state.' And she did.
She brought in a tape. To my hearing—and I have
computers in my ears, believe me—to my hearing I
was listening to Janis Joplin. She sounded so much like
Janis Joplin that I said, 'No, Cyndi, I don't think you
understand. I wanted to hear *you*. I don't want to hear
the kind of music you like, I want to hear *you*.' She
said, 'That *is* me.' I said, 'That's *you*?' I was sure it
was Janis Joplin—she fooled me completely! I said,
'Okay, now I know what I'm dealing with.' I could not
tell the difference, and I was into Joplin. I knew Joplin's stuff. I thought, if she could imitate that person
to that extent, I'm dealing with a star. I'm dealing with
an incredible voice." Joplin, she adds, had she kept
going, would have eventually lost her voice the same
way Cyndi did.

Cyndi started taking several lessons a week. With
any singer, Agresta says she has to "decide each day
what to do on the basis of what I hear. Any singer
working on their voice is going to have interference
from how they feel physically or emotionally—they

may have a fight with their boyfriend or girlfriend that'll throw them into a tailspin, whatever. The idea of training is there are so many variables—life is everywhere around you and everything affects you—so the idea is to have a way of bringing yourself to center so that you can walk onstage no matter what's going on and know exactly what's going to happen, know exactly what you're going to do. You go for a note; you know you're going to get it. It's vigorous and very physical, a lot of hard work."

Agresta says that part of a voice teacher's job is to be able to hear what a singer's voice will eventually sound like: "You always are leading the singer to a place. You're hearing what they can do today and knowing, if I just remove the tongue and get the jaw out of the way and get at this and get that loose . . . then *this* is the sound they'll be making. You're always going for the source of the sound, for the correct muscle to be making the sound. A voice teacher should be able to tell when listening to somebody how far away from that sound they are and what it's going to be like when they get there."

And she knew that Cyndi would sound great once she "got there": "Her voice," Agresta says, "is a wonderful instrument. Cyndi worked with a jazz coach before she came to me. I've heard her sing Billie Holiday music. She can sing just about anything. . . . Many singers know the melody and the lyrics and vaguely hear the band as a blur. Cyndi is not one of those people. She hears everything, knows her equipment inside and out. She knows every detail of everything. She's a singer's singer."

Cyndi worked with Agresta for nearly a year before she was ready to perform again. Of course, it's difficult for a performer with a busy schedule to continue taking lessons. How do Katie Agresta's students, if and when they hit the big time, find time for voice coaching? Simple. They take lessons over the telephone!

Says Agresta, "I have a speaker phone. I just plug it in and bring it over to the piano." She works over the phone with a number of students who are on the road a lot; she even has a student in Saint Louis who takes a regularly scheduled telephone lesson. Agresta emphasizes that telephone lessons are possible only with a longtime student whose voice she knows well.

In summary, Agresta, who in her years as a teacher has seen plenty of rock singers come and go, says, "My observation is that people who are successful in this business are really top-notch talent who have something very special to offer. There are a lot of talented people and a lot of talented voices, but there are very few people that have the whole package. The whole package is everything, plus that one thing that nobody can put their finger on. I think you could call it 'meant to be,' 'karma,' 'God-said-so,' whatever you want. It's something about the essence of that person.... I believe that a singer is a communication vehicle and that the person who's got it all together's got the business angle, the packaging, the know-how, the ability to make connections, the energy to keep at it, the ability to remember A & R men's last names and their wives' birthdays... There are a lot of people that are performers who have most of it but don't have those other things. I know Cyndi lives, breathes, eats, and sleeps this stuff—this is *it* for her.

"She has *so* much natural talent, but other than that she started with nothing, with nobody behind her. It's a Cinderella story—she made herself what she is today.

"A singer's voice," Katie Agresta concludes, "is the most precious thing they have because without it there's nothing to do in this life. What else would you want to do? If you know you can sing and it's in your blood, why would you want to do anything else?"

And so, after many months of intensive training, Cyndi was ready to face the world again. She started

KATIE AGRESTA ON VOICE TRAINING

"The difference between how I would handle an opera singer and how I'd handle a rock singer is, number one, with an opera singer I would follow the rules. It would be a very slow, very long training period—an opera singer can easily anticipate spending anywhere from eight to fifteen years in training, without blinking an eye. The idea that you would think of training any less than that is out of the question.

"A rock singer, on the other hand, has a short but very intense training period. When I work with them, I break all the rules. I don't start from point A unless they're not performing and they don't have any career pressure on them at the moment—then we can go back to the rules and go A, B, C, building one thing on top of another. But if I get somebody that's in an emergency state or somebody who's performing a lot and suddenly realizes 'Maybe I ought to get some lessons here; my performances aren't going right; my recordings aren't coming out the way they should—I'm good but I don't know what I'm doing,' that kind of thing, then I'll start by giving them a procedure to follow to get their voice ready to get on stage and something to do afterwards to calm the voice down. Give them maybe five or six kinds of exercises to get them going and to get them warmed down from a performance."

by performing a solo act at Trude Heller's on the corner of Ninth Street and Avenue of the Americas. (Don't bother looking for Trude Heller's today, by the way—it's been converted to an Italian restaurant.) As usual, she was doing other things to pay the rent.

It was around this time that attorney Ted Rosenblatt became her manager.

One evening when Cyndi was playing at Trude Heller's, Ted Rosenblatt arrived accompanied by John Turi, a songwriter and musician (sax and keyboards) who, like Cyndi, was looking for a musical partnership. Turi and Lauper became friends, started writing songs together almost immediately, and soon were putting together a new band.

Cyndi's and John Turi's musical taste at the time ran to a blend of rockabilly and good-time rock 'n' roll. They worked hard writing new songs together, poring over old songs that they might recycle, and auditioning the best musicians they could find to back them up. After a fair amount of trial and error, they had themselves a band.

They called it Blue Angel.

Blue Angel went through a number of personnel changes in the four or so years of its existence. The musicians that most fans will remember, though, are the ones appearing on the 1980 Blue Angel album: Lee Brovitz on bass, Johnny "Bullet" Morelli (formerly of the Tuff Darts) on drums, Arthur "Rockin' A" Neilson on guitar, and, of course, John Turi on keyboards and sax and Cyndi on vocals.

Not long after its formation, Blue Angel, with its unique mix of original Lauper-Turi tunes and songs from the golden days of rock 'n' roll, was booked into some of the best rock clubs in Manhattan, including the Ritz, Trax, and Privates. Cyndi had finally broken through—she was playing the songs *she* wanted to play, singing the way *she* wanted to sing, jumping around the stage the way *she* liked to jump around the stage, and dressing the way *she* liked to dress. And for the first time, people—critics, fans, music-biz types—were paying attention to her and her band.

There quickly formed a devoted coterie that followed Blue Angel from gig to gig. Just as quickly, the rumor spread that the band could be, shall we say, slightly inconsistent: If you caught them when they were *up*, they'd blow you away; but the word was that if you happened to catch them when they were *down*, you might witness them blowing themselves away—they had a tendency on those bad nights to blow their cues, trip over cables, and bump into amps and monitors.

Nevertheless, the critics agreed that Blue Angel was a force to be reckoned with. Rather, they agreed that Cyndi Lauper was one amazing performer. Robert Palmer of the *New York Times*, reviewing Blue Angel at the Ritz, wrote, "The focus of the group is Cyndi Lauper, who has a marvelous, piercing voice that sounds like a cross between Ronnie Spector and Little Eva. . . . Miss Lauper is a natural and, at her best, a riveting rock-and-roll performer. . . . her acrobatic dancing is matched only by her spectacular singing. . . . This is a high-energy band with some irresistible melodies and an exceptional lead vocalist; they are not profound, but they sure are a lot of fun."

In *Trouser Press*, Marianne Meyer waxed even more enthusiastic, writing that Cyndi ". . . looks like a teenage Miami housewife in leopardskin pants and Pebbles Flintstone strawberry blond hair, but who possesses an extraordinary set of pipes. Lauper has mastered the vanishing art of stretching one syllable into five with aching melismata derived from the Leslie Gore/Connie Francis school of girlish heartbreak. . . . When jaded critics and exhausted Friday night party-goers suddenly spring into life and dance like they mean it, you know you're listening to pop magic. This is music to snap gum by, so put on them blue suede shoes and do it!"

Variety, reviewing a Blue Angel show at the Roxy

in Los Angeles, said the band "...revives the pre-Beatles American schlock-rock era with considerable vivacity, due almost exclusively to the evocative nasality of Queens-born lead vocalist Cyndi Lauper.

"Twisting the night away in pony tail and aqua blue toreador pants, Lauper's cutting accent and wiseacre attitude are simply perfect for the music being summoned up, via both originals and oldies....Lauper's style is described by saying that her rendition of 'Lipstick on Your Collar' was letter-perfect." The folks in L.A., though, didn't seem to be too impressed—the review closes by saying that the crowd's reaction was "tepid."

On a brighter note, *Billboard* began a review of a show at the Ritz where Blue Angel opened for the Stranglers by saying that "the crowd got its money's worth, not just because of the Stranglers, but also because opening act Blue Angel was such a pleasant surprise.

"Blue Angel," the review continued presciently, "...is fronted by Cyndi Lauper, a powerful vocalist, who in the eight-song set made that band go. Possessing a voice no doubt powerful enough to shatter glass, and a happy and energetic stage presence, Lauper showed the makings of future stardom."

Just how far in the future, though, the reviewer didn't say.

BLUE ANGEL

*I*n early 1979, a young attorney named Steven Massarsky saw Blue Angel play at Trax. Massarsky had been in charge of entertainment for George McGovern's 1972 presidential campaign, had presided over the dismantling of Capricorn Records, and had managed the Allman Brothers Band for over five years; he was a music-business professional with a good eye, and ear, for talent. Blue Angel didn't look like much when he saw them—Cyndi was having one of those nights when she was constantly on the verge of falling off the stage—but when she started singing...look out!

In his television ads, Victor Kiam says his first Remington shave so impressed him that he bought the company. Well, Steve Massarsky's first close encounter with Lauper and company so impressed him that he bought the band. To be precise, he anted up five thousand dollars to buy Blue Angel's management contract from Ted Rosenblatt.

Massarsky may have been ready to unleash Blue Angel on the world, but the world wasn't quite ready for Blue Angel. Music industry pundits said more or less what they'd said a decade earlier about Janis Joplin's group, Big Brother and the Holding Company: "Incredible singer, mediocre band, mediocre material."

But Cyndi had worked hard to make Blue Angel

happen, and she wasn't about to abandon the group or the material (much of which she'd cowritten) just because people in the industry said she ought to. What did they know, anyway? After all, they were the ones who were now pressuring her to change her singing style and trade the clothes she liked for tight leather and spandex, the uniform of the late-seventies female rock 'n' roll star. Their thinking, according to Cyndi, went, "Oh, this one's selling? Let's clone her. We'll make another so-and-so." The so-and-so they wanted to model Cyndi after was either Pat Benatar, Debbie Harry, or, believe it or not, Barbra Streisand, depending on which pundit was offering the advice. "They wanted to turn me into Barbra Streisand," Cyndi insists, "put cement go-go boots on me so I couldn't do anything onstage."

Cyndi told them all to take a hike.

CYNDI ON BEING A NATURAL ROCK 'N' ROLLER

"You're going for a basic gut emotion, so you do what comes from the gut."

Katie Agresta, who has seen many bands—including Blue Angel—come together and break up, has her own perspective on the situation. "Singers get very attached to being in a band," she says, "and they love their band members. When you make music together like that and you write together and you perform together and you suffer together, there's a bond. It's very hard to break up a band. They believe in themselves. They believe they have something really special. When a record company says, 'We just want *you*; the rest of you go home,' it can just make a singer crazy. Some people handle it by firing the band: 'Oh, well, where do I sign.' And some people don't. They just can't."

Said Cyndi, "When you're a girl and have a big voice, there are all these jerks who'll come up to you and say, 'We're gonna build a band around *you*! You're gonna be *the star*!' Me and John always wanted a *band*."

Blue Angel and Cyndi stuck to their guns and continued playing gigs, writing songs, rehearsing, improving. Their local popularity with fans and critics continued to grow, although they were still barely eking out a living. (They were eking out their living either playing on their own or opening for the likes of Joe Jackson, the Ramones, and Steve Forbert.) As Cyndi says, "You have to be willing to stand by your convictions. And starve. We starved."

Then, late in 1979, Blue Angel passed another milestone: They signed a recording contract with Polydor, a division of giant Polygram Records. It looked like this was going to be the big break—the record company seemed intent on doing a first-class job producing and promoting the album. After a short search for a producer, which included an ill-fated meeting between Cyndi and Georgio Moroder, producer of the disco hits that made Donna Summer famous, everyone agreed that Roy Halee, producer of Simon and Garfunkel's top-selling albums in the sixties, was right for the job.

The album, eponymously entitled *Blue Angel*, was released by Polydor in 1980. (A single of "I Had a Love" followed.) No one hearing it for the first time could have mistaken it for a disco record: It was entirely free of the "wall-of-sound" and the lushly synthesized production associated with much of the music of the late seventies and early eighties. In fact, it was more closely related to twelve-bar, three-chord Carl Perkins or early Elvis Presley or to the sound of the great girl groups than to Donna Summer and Georgio Moroder. In short, it was pure and simple rock 'n' roll.

Of the twelve tunes on the album, ten were home-grown Lauper-Turi or Lauper-Turi-and-Company compositions. Here's a rundown of the songs:

SIDE ONE:

"MAYBE HE'LL KNOW" by CYNDI LAUPER AND JOHN TURI. When you talk to Blue Angel fans today, the song they invariably mention first is "Maybe He'll Know." Most of them, in fact, think that this song was released as a single, which it wasn't. Why does everyone remember "Maybe He'll Know"? Simple: It's a great song. Built around a classic one-six-four-five chord progression, with direct, uncomplicated lyrics and a straight-on arrangement featuring Turi on organ, Clavinette, and saxophone, it's one of those tunes you might hear once and find yourself humming weeks later.

As with many memorable songs, "Maybe He'll Know" presents one simple idea through its lyrics. Actually, the idea is presented by the title of the song: Maybe he'll know that I love him. The lyrics go on to restate the idea, or rhetorical statement, adding only the worry that he might *not* ever know or that if he does know, he might take too long about it. The song's great accomplishment lyrically is to slip the phrase "I've got this anxious feeling" into the chorus. This is a line that no self-respecting rock 'n' roll songwriter who preceded Lauper and Turi ever had the nerve to use. Somehow, Lauper and Turi managed to pull it off.

"I HAD A LOVE" by CYNDI LAUPER AND JOHN TURI. This was the A side of Blue Angel's only single. Although there's a lot of tropical stuff going on in this cut—castanets, tambourines, rattling gourds—it has the overall feel of a girl-group song. To be specific, it feels like something by the Crystals—you half expect the first words to be "See the way he walks down the street/Watch the way he shuffles his feet..." (the opening line of "He's a Rebel," the number one song of 1962). It also feels a lot like "This Magic Moment," a 1960 song by the Drifters. So: a Caribbean girl-group–doo-wop sound as interpreted by a young woman from Ozone Park.

What's amazing about it is that it works!

In addition to the tropical percussion sounds, there's some great foursquare chord banging on the acoustic piano, in addition to a thin, ethereal organ line floating on top of everything else; there's also a keen, slicing Neilson guitar solo. In the deep background, the boys croon "ooo-wahs" behind Cyndi's mournful singing.

What is the song about? A good question. It seems that the singer was in love once—she "had a lifetime in a moment"—but made the oft-repeated mistake of forgetting to mention her feelings to the guy. Now, much later, she's decided that those were the days (or that was the moment) and that it's about time she told him. Of course, being a little mixed up, she only addresses him directly (when *you* were mine) in the choruses; in the verses she talks about him in the third person (when *he* was mine). By the end, she seems resigned to reliving that terrific moment for the rest of her life. Another rock 'n' roll tragedy.

"FADE" by CYNDI LAUPER AND JOHN TURI. The key line in this song is "Never thought I'd be so proud, thought I would never live without you . . . Fade!" The key sound is Cyndi's exuberant "uh-oh-oh-oh"— she's so happy she's rid of the guy!

As with all Blue Angel tunes, the lyrics are simple. The singer is walking down a street that she "guesses" is the street where her ex resides. She looks up at his window and, attempting mind control, tries to get him to fade away. That's all there is to it. It's one of the happiest "drop dead—I don't need you" songs you'll ever hear. Cyndi's final "Fade!" is devastating.

Musically, "Fade" is completely straightforward: organ, guitar, bass, drums. Parts of Lee Brovitz's bass line, by the way, could have been lifted right out of an early-sixties surfing instrumental, the Chantays' "Pipeline," for example, or the Surfaris' "Wipe Out."

"ANNA BLUE" by CYNDI LAUPER AND JOHN TURI. The first thing you notice about "Anna Blue" is that it opens with a tricky time-signature change: two bars of six/eight followed by one bar of two/eight. Despite this, the song sounds a lot more like Leslie Gore than like the Mahavishnu Orchestra. No, this is unfair to the song—it may have the feel of a lesser-known Leslie Gore tune but with a much more sophisticated and interesting sound.

The song, like so many on *Blue Angel*, is addressed to, or is about, someone other than the person singing the words. In this case, the subject portrayed is Anna Blue. What does the portrait tell us about this Anna Blue? That she's a small-town girl who aspires to be part of the big-town scene and that when all is said and done, this aspiration can come to no good.

One of the key lines, "You can wear it with a smile, you can wear it with a style," would appear to apply to Anna's dreams. A discussion on the subject of how anyone can wear a dream, with or without a smile, is well outside the scope of this book; suffice it to say that the lyrics are all the way over on the impressionistic side of the scale. They sound fine when Cyndi's singing them, though, which is what makes them work as well as they do.

Musically, the high points are a beautiful keening John Turi sax solo and Cyndi's vocal at the end, which floats beautifully over that six/eight-six/eight-two/eight time.

"CAN'T BLAME ME" by CYNDI LAUPER AND JOHN TURI. The opening bars have a real Buddy Holly feel to them, as does the little twist Cyndi gives to the word "know" at the beginning of the first chorus. John Turi's got an interesting sax solo in this one—it starts out sounding like Daddy G, goes through a brief series of John Coltrane–Ornette Coleman barks and squeaks, then comes back to earth.

This song delivers a really happy, upbeat, "I love you" message; it's an attempt to wheedle and cajole some love out of the boy, who, evidently, has been saving it for a special occasion. The boy's a little obstinate, unfortunately—he "doesn't want to know" about this love thing, and the singer'll promise him just about anything to get his attention.

We never do learn whether or not Cyndi gets through to the guy, but we can assume that if he knows anything about music, he'll be reciprocating her affection momentarily.

"LATE" by CYNDI LAUPER, JOHN TURI, AND LEE BROVITZ. This is definitely the cutest song on the Blue Angel album. There have been several other "late" songs in the history of rock, most notably the Everly Brothers' "Wake Up Little Suzie," the number one hit of 1957, and Ricky Nelson's "It's Late" from 1959, but these songs differ from Blue Angel's "Late" in one important respect. In the old days, when you sang about being late, you were probably referring to being out on a date, getting stuck somewhere (possibly because you were indulging in proscribed activities such as heavy petting in the back seat of Dad's car), and getting busted by the ultimate authority figures: your parents and your date's parents. In the aftermath of this debacle, you would probably also be stigmatized or ridiculed by the other kids. ("What're we gonna tell your momma? What're we gonna tell your pop? What're we gonna tell our friends when they say 'Ooh, la la?!'" is the way the Everlys summed up the problem.)

The situation in "Late" is quite different. Here Cyndi is offering a bubbly apology to her dreamboat because she's late for a date. There's nothing ominous going on here, no authority figures to worry about, no friends looking for gossip, not even a problem with the boyfriend—Cyndi's confident that he's going to love her whether or not she gets there on time. The closest Cyndi comes to getting heavy in this little number is when she makes this universal observation: "Ticketytock, whew, the clock it don't stop, it don't stop, it don't stop!"

Musically, "Late" is a classic rocker, with some hot "Rockin' A" Neilson by-way-of Chuck Berry guitar playing and some fancy John Turi by-way-of Little Richard piano playing. There's also a great trick ending and a bunch of Cyndi's soaring "uh-oh"s.

SIDE TWO:

"CUT OUT" by KING/MACK/FOWLER. The only instrumental on the album, "Cut Out," harks back to the great instrumental bands of the late fifties and early sixties—Johnny and the Hurricanes, the Champs, Duane Eddy and the Rebels, Booker T. and the MGs, the Ventures. It starts with a drum intro that could be right out of Sandy Nelson's 1961 hit "Let There Be Drums," then quickly segues into an arrangement that sounds like a cross between the Champs mellow "Tequila" (1958) and one of the more frenetic numbers from Johnny and the Hurricanes, "Red River Rock" (1959), for example.

Cyndi sits this one out as the boys sing the only line in the song: "Cut out, cut out." The instrumental highlight is John Turi's sax playing, which is in the wild, wailing style of Johnny and the Hurricanes' John Paris.

"TAKE A CHANCE" by CYNDI LAUPER AND JOHN TURI. This is the B side of Blue Angel's single. "Take a Chance" has more genuine rockabilly feel to it than any other cut on the album—it doesn't have a trace of the girl-group sound. Cyndi is in the rockabilly mode right from the beginning, with her whispered "Go cat, go cat," which evokes Carl Perkins's "It's one for the money, two for the show, three to get ready, now go, cat, go!" at the beginning of "Blue Suede Shoes." Even Cyndi's vocal inflections have a country-rockabilly sound to them—she doesn't say "me," she says "may," as in "take a chance with may."

The song is a happy upbeat play for a very cool guy, the kind of guy who walks into a room with a curled-up smile on his lips. (Cyndi might have been thinking of Elvis here—he was the king of the curled-up smile.) When she talks about running her fingers through his hair, you just know that if she ever gets that far with him, she's going to need a beach towel to clean the Brylcreem off her hands.

There's a low "dum da dum da dum" bass vocal running through the song (this, actually, is more in the style of the Coasters than, say, the Jordanaires, who backed up Elvis Presley, but it seems to work just fine), a lot of honky-tonk piano and cool sax from Turi, and some nice, twangy, Duane-Eddy-style guitar throughout—except in the instrumental section, where guitarist Neilson plays a clean, old-fashioned rockabilly guitar solo over a shuffle beat. There are also a bunch of terrific "oop"s from Cyndi. All in all, "Take a Chance" is lots of fun.

"JUST THE OTHER DAY" by CYNDI LAUPER AND JOHN TURI. More castanets and tambourines, with a steel drum sound during the instrumental break. "Just the Other Day" is another Blue Angel song with a calypso–girl-group feel—something like a cross between Jimmy Cliff and the Shangri-Las.

The lyrics are addressed to a guy who has just been given the ditch by his girlfriend. The singer—we'll call her Cyndi—who seems to be friends with the girl who's given the guy the heave, is trying to figure out exactly what happened: "Did she let you go?" As she hears his side of the story, she seems to be getting more and more interested in him. Finally she asks, "Will you still talk to me" if she—the other girlfriend—is no longer in the picture. It could be the start of a beautiful relationship.

With Cyndi singing at the top of her form and some wonderful girl-group background vocals and harmonies, the song is one of the richest and most enjoyable on *Blue Angel*.

"I'M GONNA BE STRONG" by BARRY MANN AND CYNTHIA WEIL. This song is a beautiful, touching ballad about the demise of a romance. In the first verse, Cyndi's singing is sweet and sad; by the end of the second verse she's beginning to toughen up and let 'er rip; by the end of the song she's pulled out all the stops—it's hard to believe what she can do! Her final "cry" is a real speaker-shatterer.

Barry Mann and Cynthia Weil, who wrote "I'm Gonna Be Strong" for Gene Pitney, were one of the premier songwriting teams of the late fifties and early sixties. They worked in New York's Brill Building along with many of the best songwriters of the time—Neil Sedaka, Carole King, Gerry Goffin, Jeff Barry, Ellie Greenwich, Mike Stoller and Jerry Lieber, and others. Among the hits penned by the Mann-Weil team were "Uptown" and "He's Sure the Boy I Love" by the Crystals, "Johnny Loves Me" by Shelley Fabares, "I'll Take You Home" and "Saturday Night at the Movies" by the Drifters, "You've Lost That Lovin' Feeling" (cowritten with producer Phil Spector) and "(You're My) Soul And Inspiration" by the Righteous Brothers, and "We Gotta Get Outta This Place" by Eric Burdon and the Animals. It's great to hear Cyndi sing one of their songs.

"LORRAINE" by CYNDI LAUPER AND JOHN TURI. The singer is telling the very simple story of how, long ago, "a lonely man" fell in love with a woman named Lorraine, to whom the song is addressed. It appears to be raining at the time this story is being told; the refrain of the rain falls mainly on Lorraine.

Cyndi's voice is in good form here, with a nice, biting quality toward the end. The instrumental section sounds a lot like "Sleep Walk" by Santo and Johnny, which happened to be the number one song of 1959. How about that?

"EVERYBODY'S GOT AN ANGEL" by BLUE ANGEL AND HENRY GROSS. Cyndi does some flat-out, vocal-chord–poppin' shouting on the last song on the album. Lyrically, this is one of the most basic songs of all time, saying nothing more than don't worry. Don't hurry. You're gonna find someone because "every-body's got an angel." Johnny "Bullet" Morelli keeps pushing with his hard-driving drums, Arthur Neilson produces some more twangy sounds with the fat strings of his guitar, Lee Brovitz's staccato bass playing provides a bouncy bottom, and John Turi keeps the top swirling with filmy organ glissandos. It's a nice, smooth, fast rocker that makes you want to jump up and dance.

Blue Angel, as everyone by now knows, was not a commercially successful album. Why? We'll never know all the reasons, but many in the industry agree with those critics who were quick to point out that some of the songs on the album tend to sound like rehashed fifties material. John Young, writing in *Trouser Press*, was typical of the critics who didn't care for the album. His review, from the January 1981 issue, reads, "Shoop, shoop anyone? Blue Angel wants to synthesize golden debris into something 'new' the way Blondie did, only with more of an accent on '50s grease. Cyndi Lauper's self-conscious vocal mannerisms are good for starters; the others need to learn how to cut loose."

In the album's defense, it must be said that despite the occasional thinness of the sound, despite its occasional lapses into déjà vu, many of the songs are fun to listen to, Cyndi's singing is a treat, and the playing is fine, tight, and clean. Morelli on drums and Brovitz on bass provide a solid rhythmic spine, Neilson's guitar work, sparse and tasty, has been affectionately described as "Chuck Berry goes surfing," and Turi's keyboard and sax work was just what the doctor ordered—again, check out his saxophone solo on "Anna Blue."

And some critics had good things to say about the album. According to a recent issue of *Rolling Stone*, Cyndi "...came as close to the girl-group grail as is probably possible with the breathtaking 'Maybe He'll Know.'" In a piece written around the time the album was first released, *Rolling Stone*'s Christopher Connelly quoted Cyndi as saying, "If you're gonna make something new, go back to the beginning and create from the base." Connelly approved, comparing Cyndi to Ronnie Spector and other great female rockers. *Blue Angel* may not have been the best first album ever produced, but all in all it was a better-than-average debut.

What did Cyndi think of the album? While she was not unhappy about the way the album *sounded*, she did not like the way it *looked* or at least the way *she* looked on the jacket—she insisted that her picture was the spitting image of Big Bird! (Many fans liked the cover with its nice, bright colors and funny hand-tinted photos of the band members. The *New York Times* reviewer, on the other hand, said, "On the cover of their first album, Blue Angel looked like yet another slick, shallow power-pop band. . . ." As always, there's no disputing taste.) Cyndi was equally unhappy with the layout of the liner notes on the record slipcover. At first she wanted to trash the jacket and slipcover and design new ones, but a move like that would have cost more money than Polydor was willing to spend on a new, unproven group. And so the album was released with a cover Cyndi hated, making her even more determined to have complete artistic control over her future projects.

Blue Angel's local fans snapped up the record, but local fans do not a hit make. It sold in the neighborhood of twelve thousand copies and was difficult to find outside of selected record stores in and around New York City. In Cyndi's words, it "went lead." Nearly four years later, when *She's So Unusual* started its climb to the top of the charts, Polydor rereleased the Blue Angel album with a big Featuring Cyndi Lauper sticker on the cover. It is rumored to have sold over fifteen thousand copies in the first half of 1984 alone. Isn't it amazing what a few years and a sticker can do?

Having an album out did help Blue Angel for a while. They made three early videos with director Ed Griles, one of which won a Creative Short Award at the New York Film Festival. Unfortunately, as this was before the advent of MTV, very few people actually saw the films. (Griles and Lauper were destined to work together again—on the "Girls Just Want to Have Fun," "Time after Time," and "She Bop" videos.) Later in 1980, the year the album came out, Blue Angel was Joe Jackson's opening act on a tour of Germany; they also appeared on German television with Hall and Oates. Nevertheless, times were still tough back home as the band continued to struggle on the New York club circuit. "We were starving," Cyndi told *New York* magazine. "We used to go to a gig and look at the deli tray as the meal for the day. We'd look at each other and say, 'Is this really happening to us?'"

Unfortunately, it was.

CYNDI SOLO

After parting company with Polydor and subsequently with Blue Angel as well, due to mounting business pressures and to declining creativity, Cyndi signed to Portrait Records as a solo artist in the spring of 1983.

From a Portrait Records press release

Well, it wasn't quite that simple. One of Blue Angel's biggest problems always had been that few people outside of hard-core fans seemed to understand what they were trying to do. Among those who didn't understand—at least as far as Cyndi was concerned—were the people at Polydor. "It was before the rockabilly boom," she says, "and it was before MTV. We were branded as a fifties group. We were actually a hybrid of Elvis Presley riffs, kitschy, self-realization lyrics of my feelings as a woman of the eighties, and my voice, which has been called a cross between Brenda Lee and Ronnie Spector." ·

"SHE'S LIKE A YOUNG LUCILLE BALL ON SPEED...."

It doesn't happen with every new star on the rock 'n' roll horizon, but for some reason it did, and still does, with Cyndi: She's constantly being compared with other singers, other celebrities, and even with cartoon characters. In fact, Cyndi's probably the first singer in history to feel obliged to tell *Rolling Stone* that she's definitely *not* a cartoon.

Since you can't always tell the players without a scorecard, here is a guide to the people, real and imaginary, with whom Cyndi's been compared.

Other Singers

They may not always be on target, but at least these are comparisons with real people who sing.

RONNIE SPECTOR: The full name of the Ronettes' first album is ... *Presenting the Fabulous RONETTES Featuring VERONICA.* Veronica, Ronnie. It's her voice that grabs you on the great Ronettes hits "Be My Baby" and "Baby I Love You" and "(The Best Part of) Breakin' Up," all from the early sixties. And, yes, there is more than a hint of her voice in Cyndi's ... and there ain't nothin' wrong with that!

BRENDA LEE was a pint-sized country singer who in the late fifties was thrust into the role of a rocker and rose to the occasion. Her calling card was a powerful, personality-packed voice that could make 'em cry with a song like "I Want to be Wanted" or make 'em laugh with a song like "Sweet Nothin's." On a slow song from *She's So Unusual*, "Time after Time," for example, Cyndi's vocal colorations are sometimes reminiscent of Brenda Lee's rockabilly stylings.

CONNIE FRANCIS also appeared in the late fifties, recording such hits as "Among My Souvenirs," "Stupid Cupid," "Where the Boys Are," and "Lipstick on Your Collar" (which Cyndi used to perform with her band Blue Angel). It's not *that* easy to hear the Francis influence in Cyndi's singing, but if you listen hard enough, who knows what you'll come up with?

LESLIE GORE: Remember "It's My Party"? "Judy's Turn to Cry"? "You Don't Own Me"? They were all by lachrymose Leslie Gore, the undisputed queen of sob rock. It's not that Cyndi sounds like Leslie Gore, but you can tell that somewhere or other she likes the *idea* of Leslie Gore. Would she have done "Money Changes Everything" if she didn't?

LITTLE EVA, one of the few one-woman girl groups, is best known for her great dance tune "The Loco-Motion." Robert Palmer of the *New York Times*, exercising his First Amendment right of free speech, once suggested that Cyndi sounds like a cross between Ronnie Spector and Little Eva.

MELANIE came along in the late sixties with a song that rarely appears in jukeboxes these days, "Brand New Key." Her voice was raspy, her material on the saccharine side. Cyndi doesn't really sound like her; the reason certain critics have said she does is that Cyndi is capable of making her voice sound just about any way she wants it to sound. One of the sounds she gets has a raspy edge to it. Melanie is remembered for her raspiness. That's the connection.

Celebrity Comparisons

"SHE'S LIKE A YOUNG LUCILLE BALL ON SPEED" is one of the ways David Hinckley, of the New York *Daily News*, describes Cyndi in concert.

It's hard to say how accurate this is—Cyndi is certainly a *colorful* and *dynamic* performer, with a *unique voice* and a highly developed *sense of humor*, but whether she evokes the image, say, of Lucy on her hands and knees in the kitchen, yelling something like "Riiiicky! There are *three thousand five hundred and sixty-two tiles* on this floor!" is anybody's guess.

THE YOUNG SHIRLEY TEMPLE is an entertainer whose voice Cyndi's resembles. Or so opines Stephen Holden of the *New York Times.* Perhaps he meant the young Shirley Temple *on speed*, which would make a lot more sense.

BERNADETTE PETERS is an obvious choice; after all, she's from Ozone Park, too.

GRACIE ALLEN, as in *Newsweek*'s phrase, "The Gracie Allen of Rock." Allen, George Burns's wife and comedy partner, was the scatterbrained master of the non sequitur and the oxymoron. Despite Cyndi's claim that she's a singer, not a comedienne, she's one of the funniest talk-show guests around. *Newsweek* just might be right.

PIA ZADORA the actress became Pia Zadora the rock star by recording a duet and filming a video clip entitled "When the Rain Begins to Fall," with Jermaine Jackson. While it has been suggested by a few reporters that from certain angles Cyndi and Pia reflect light in a similar manner, most people feel either that this is a hallucination or that those angles exist but are awfully dangerous.

Cartoon Characters

BETTY BOOP, the doll-like singer with the oop-oop-a-doo voice, has been animating audiences for over fifty years. Betty's style is more Depression modern that new wave, but her heart's in the right place. Reporters in search of a way to describe Cyndi's speaking voice are thankful to Max Fleischer,

Betty's creator, and to Helen Kane, the actual singer after whom Betty was modeled.

OLIVE OYL, Popeye's number one gal, is another Max Fleischer creation. Mae Questel, the real person who did Olive Oyl's voice, was also the voice behind Betty Boop, so it's not unreasonable that Olive also reminds people of Cyndi. (Cyndi would never put up with a guy like Popeye, though—he's no fun!)

"LIKE A CARTOON MOUSE" is the way one rock journalist describes the way Cyndi speaks. This is not a very good description. After all, we don't know *which* cartoon mouse the journalist is referring to, and whether it's a normal cartoon mouse or a three hundred pounder. Back to the drawing board!

"LIKE TWEETY BIRD WITH A HEAVY NEW YORK ACCENT" is another rock scribe's cartoon simile. Much better—at least we know which cartoon bird we're dealing with. However, Tweety has a noticeable speech impediment, which Cyndi most certainly does not. No wonder she's sick of being compared to cartoon characters.

Being classified as "retro rockers" meant that radio stations, which had gradually locked themselves in programming straitjackets, wouldn't touch Blue Angel with a ten-foot antenna. No radio play meant no new fans except for those who managed to see the group play live. No new fans meant no record sales. No record sales meant no radio play. It was a vicious circle, and it was making Cyndi and the other band members very unhappy.

Whether or not Polydor supported the album the way they should have depends on whom you are speaking with. While Cyndi felt that the label was largely to blame for the record's lack of success, there are those in the industry who claim that Polydor spent upward of a quarter of a million dollars—no mean sum on an unknown group—producing and distributing the album, publicizing the band, taking them on tour, and generally trying to make Blue Angel fly. At some point, of course, it's all academic: Regardless of whose fault it was, the album just wasn't destined to make it to the top ten.

Cyndi wasn't pleased with the thought that Blue Angel had a contractual obligation to cut another album for Polydor. Before it was time to start booking a studio, however, there was a major upheaval at the record company and several of the top executives with whom Cyndi and the band had been dealing left Polydor. Blue Angel, in the ensuing confusion, convinced the label that neither side would benefit from a continuation of the relationship. The contractual obligation, to Cyndi's relief, was dissolved.

It was now 1982. Blue Angel was still struggling along, without a record contract, with little recognition and few prospects. "Things just didn't work out well with us," Cyndi says of that difficult time, "and the chemistry slowly deteriorated until it became a futile effort—a negative process—to stay together." To add to their problems, Cyndi had concluded that she'd outgrown manager Massarsky. Finally, in a sort of spectacular crash landing, the band fired Massarsky, who turned around and sued for reimbursement of the eighty thousand dollars he reportedly had spent on them over the years.

It was the end of the line for Blue Angel. Not only did the band break up, but Cyndi, among others, filed for bankruptcy. It was granted in early 1983.

Although Cyndi was temporarily bandless, she kept very busy between the demise of Blue Angel and her signing on as a solo artist with Portrait. Continuing her tradition of taking weird jobs to pay the rent, she found employment at Miho, a Japanese piano bar near Manhattan's theater district. Cyndi's job description was something in the neighborhood of "performing geisha."

The job consisted of singing classics like "I Can't Go for That (No Can Do)," singing Japanese songs phonetically, and dancing with the inebriated businessmen who patronized the place. This was not Cyndi's idea of a good way for a girl to have fun. "It was breaking my heart, I was so depressed," she told *Rolling Stone*. "I don't even like to have someone put his hand on mine if I don't know him. I felt like a dance-hall girl."

In addition to working at Miho, she also worked for a time at Screaming Mimi's, a store on the Upper West Side specializing in the sort of vintage clothing that Cyndi loves to wear.

She also continued her voice lessons with Katie Agresta.

She also cut a number of demo tracks, produced by rock perennial Rick Derringer.

She also embarked on a search for a new manager. Finding a manager presented a major challenge. As Cyndi puts it, "I would visit a manager and go home and have nightmares about him."

Cyndi tells a story about how around this time she went through a period when she occasionally heard a voice in her head saying, "Find Dave, find Dave." At the time, she didn't know anyone named Dave. Then one night a guy stepped up to her and said, "Hi, my name's Dave." It was David Wolff, who happened to be a rock 'n' roll manager. "I met Dave on Pearl Harbor Day in 1981, and we became friends," Cyndi reminisces. "From that there came a relationship, and then he became my manager."

Wolff, it so happened, was about to start his own management company. At first she wasn't sure if she wanted to be managed by a man with whom she was having a relationship. Then she realized, "...he's a trustworthy fellow and a great manager, so it would have been stupid not to." Soon they were sharing an apartment in Manhattan's East Fifties, just Cyndi, Dave, and Cyndi's plants, which have names like Chrissie, Greenie, Spidee, and Bertha. The arrangement, according to Cyndi, has worked out superbly. "It could be great or horrible to have your manager as your boyfriend, but so far it's been great." (In addition to Cyndi, Wolff manages the Major Thinkers, one of Cyndi's favorite groups and her frequent opening act in live performances.)

If you're wondering what Dave Wolff looks like, just think back on the "Time after Time" video. Dave played the part of—you guessed it—Cyndi's boyfriend. (The video depicts a relationship breaking up, but don't worry—in real life everything's going just fine.)

And so, with the support of a new manager who also happened to be her boyfriend, Cyndi was ready to get her career rolling again.

David Wolff's band ArcAngel (no relation to Blue Angel) already had a deal with Portrait Records, a subsidiary of CBS Epic, so it was natural for Wolff to introduce his new client to his contacts there. Wolff knew that Portrait would be the ideal label for Cyndi to sign with—it was small enough to give her the personal attention she needed, and yet as part of CBS, perhaps the world's most successful record company, it had the resources to back up an album with the right kind of advertising, publicity, and distribution.

Wolff's feelings about Portrait were well founded, and the Portrait people proved to be shrewd judges of talent: In early 1983 they signed Cyndi Lauper to a recording contract and began making plans for her first solo album, the album that would be known as *She's So Unusual*.

Lennie Petze, head of Portrait Records, took a personal interest in the project, introducing Cyndi to producer Rick Chertoff. Chertoff, having just produced an album for Saturday Night Live mainstay Joe Piscopo, was eager to do an album with a singer. The timing was perfect.

Chertoff is a producer known for his uncanny musical "matchmaking" abilities—introducing compatible musicians to each other and introducing the right song to the right artist. On Cyndi's album, he came through on both counts. It can even be argued that he made a match between the music of two *cities*, New York and Philadelphia.

Eric Bazilian and Rob Hyman, formerly of Baby Grand, now of the Hooters, were in the forefront of the Philly connection. On the liner notes of *She's So Unusual*, the three musicians who received top-credit, bold-type listings are Cyndi Lauper, Eric Bazilian, and Rob Hyman; everyone else is listed under Additional Musicians. Bazilian is credited with singing background vocals and playing guitars, bass guitar, hooter (a little-known cross between a harmonica and a piano), and saxophone; Hyman is credited with singing background vocals and playing keyboards. Hyman and Bazilian, along with Cyndi and Rick Chertoff, are also given credit for arranging all the songs with the exception of "When You Were Mine."

The other leading member of the Philly connection is Robert Hazard, who wrote "Girls Just Want to Have Fun," the first single to be released from the album.

"Girls Just Want to Have Fun" is an excellent example of Chertoff's matchmaking abilities. Long before he was enlisted to produce Cyndi's album, Chertoff had heard the song performed by Hazard. Chertoff knew it was a catchy number—it had to be to stick in his head as long as it did—but it wasn't until he met Cyndi that he knew what to do with it.

Cyndi recalls that when she first heard Hazard's song, she was not impressed—it seemed to her to be an ode to sexism. "It was originally about how fortunate he was 'cause he was a guy around these girls who wanted to have 'fun'—with *him*—*down there*, of which we do not speak lest we go blind." Chertoff, according to Cyndi, still felt that the *idea* of the song was right for her, but it took her a while to come around. "What am I supposed to do?" she said. "Dance the cancan and say 'I'm so dumb, I'm so dumb'?"

On further reflection, though, she realized that by adapting the lyrics, she could make the song suit her own purposes. With a few deft strokes of her pen, the song was transformed into the magnificent, happy, liberating anthem that would soon catch the world's fancy and make Cyndi Lauper a household word. On the album liner notes, Cyndi thanks Robert Hazard "for letting me change your song."

Since "Girls Just Want to Have Fun" became such a big hit for Cyndi, both as a single and as a twelve-inch dance single, as one of the cornerstones of the album's success, and as her first music video, and since it will always be remembered as her first big solo smash, it might be edifying to spend a few moments looking at the songwriter, Robert Hazard.

ROBERT HAZARD:
A CAPSULE BIOGRAPHY

1979: A Philadelphia jewelry engraver named Robert Hazard, then in his mid-twenties, quits his job and starts to live out his lifelong dream of being a rock 'n' roll star. He puts together a band called the Heroes and starts playing wherever and whenever he can in the Philadelphia–Southern New Jersey–Delaware Valley area. He quickly gains a local following. With what little money he is able to accumulate, he produces his own records in limited quantities and distributes them locally.

1981: A local FM radio station decides that Hazard is going to be big—they start playing his records in the regular rotation. Hazard rises to the occasion by recording and releasing a great two-sided single, "Escalator of Life" backed with "Change Reaction." To everyone's surprise, over fifty thousand copies are sold. *Rolling Stone* proclaims Hazard and the Heroes "a rock 'n' roll event waiting to happen."

1982: Hazard releases an EP, or "mini-LP," called *Robert Hazard* containing four of his own compositions—"Change Reaction," "Escalator of Life," "Hang Around with You," and "Out of the Blue," plus a cover of Bob Dylan's "Blowin' in the Wind." He signs a contract with RCA, who remixes the record and distributes over eighty-five thousand copies nationally.

1984: Hazard's first RCA album, the lushly produced *Wing of Fire*, is released. The album, which consists mainly of slow, moody songs as opposed to out-and-out rockers, is met with mixed reviews (although many critics flip for "Interplanetary Private Eye"), but Hazard himself is compared to Bruce Springsteen, Dion DiMucci of Dion and the Belmonts, Felix Cavaliere of the Young Rascals, and even to David Bowie.

Notes on "Girls Just Want to Have Fun": Hazard has performed "Girls" in concert, but he has never recorded the song (except on demo tapes). According to Alan Spielman, his comanager, he probably never will.

Hazard is planning a second album with RCA; he'll probably produce this one himself to get back to the simpler, harder sound he had on the EP. In addition to recording a number of tracks for possible inclusion in "The Wild Life," a movie written by "Fast Times at Ridgemont High" author Cameron Crowe, he has given several tunes to Kenny Rogers, who's considering them for his next album. In summary, it looks like we'll be hearing more from the writer of "Girls Just Want to Have Fun."

And, oh yes—just as Cyndi thanks Robert Hazard for letting her change his song, Robert Hazard thanks Cyndi for making such a big hit out of it. He really does.

SHE'S SO
UNUSUAL

"**O**n the record I tried to cover all human emotions," Cyndi said after *She's So Unusual* was released. "It was a chance to take, and I wanted to take it, because music without courage is not worth doing. I became a musician so that I could be happy and do what I love to do in life: write and sing. You can take a stab at doing something totally different and get killed for it. But at least it's *real*. And people feel all different ways: People feel happy, people feel sad."

One of the things that made Cyndi feel sad back in the Flyer days was that she was stuck covering other people's songs and didn't get to do any of her own material. In retrospect, maybe the problem wasn't so much that she was covering other people's material as that someone else was choosing the material for her. As she explains in a Portrait press release,

> I decided to just go ahead and do it [her solo album], though I hadn't written many new songs—I had broken up my partnership with John Turi—and didn't like the idea of just singing other people's songs. But for *She's So Unusual*, producer Rick Chertoff and I selected songs that enabled me to keep my integrity and that meant something to me. I wrote some too.

She certainly did—*She's So Unusual* contains four songs that list Cyndi as coauthor: the haunting ballad behind her second video clip, "Time after Time," by Cyndi and Rob Hyman; "She Bop," her third video, by Cyndi, S. Lunt, G. Corbett and Rick Chertoff; "Witness" by Cyndi and her old partner John Turi; and "I'll Kiss You" by Cyndi and Jules Shear.

Here's a quick rundown of all the songs on the album:

SIDE ONE:

"MONEY CHANGES EVERYTHING" by TOM GRAY. Gray was the brain behind the Brains, an ill-fated postpunk band from Atlanta that produced and released a homemade version of "Money Changes Everything" in 1978. The record got the group a contract with a major record company, but it didn't help: They broke up shortly thereafter. According to rock critic Greil Marcus, the Brains' version of the song "opens with a woman leaving her man for a prospect with a thicker wallet. Gray sings as the man; with right on his side, he wins your sympathy automatically, puts you in the song. Lauper sings as the woman. . . . 'It's all in the past now,' runs the most chilling line of the song, even worse than that gruesomely frigid 'yeah' in the fourth line, which is no happy improvisation: Gray wrote it. He gave the word a sardonic curl; Lauper seems to dump her childhood in the course of saying it."

Musically, Cyndi's version of "Money Changes Everything" contains a striking dual-synthesizer line that runs through most of the song. The synths are there on the eight-bar intro, then cut out while Cyndi sings the first verse backed by a basic rock backbone of guitar, bass, and drums. On the last word of the verse, however, the word "money," the synths reappear. The sound of those synthesizers is fuzzy, soft, comfortable. If a mink coat were a musical instrument, that's what it would sound like. Through the rest of the tune, except for the second verse, which drops back to the guitar-bass-drums configuration, Cyndi's voice (which has a rough, street-punk quality in this song—listen to the way she swallows the *t* in the word "waitin'" in the second line) is wrapped in the insulating, furry sound of those synths. The instrumental section starts with just drums and a very plaintive hooter, later joined by a simple rhythm guitar; it's as if the song is undergoing a moral crisis, a reaction against the rich furriness of what's gone before. Then Cyndi ("Yeah! Yeah! Yeah!!") charges back in, wrapped in her purring synths, and forever seals her fate: goodbye naked simplicity; hello furs, hello insulation, hello money.

"GIRLS JUST WANT TO HAVE FUN" by ROBERT HAZARD. There have always been rock 'n' roll songs limning the traditional conflict between teenagers and authority figures. What's different about "Girls Just Want to Have Fun" is that this time the kid not only gets her way, but she liberates her uptight parents to boot. (We never do learn what happens to the anonymous, almost unmentionable boys who like to lock beautiful girls away from the rest of the world.) Of course, the lyrics don't really tell us that the heroine liberates her parents. They only show us the parents hurling a few clichés at their daughter to express their displeasure at the hours she keeps, followed by the daughter's lighthearted responses. What's interesting, and moving, about the response is that it's the daughter, our heroine, who has all the creative energy in the family—she's the one who's doing all the jumping around and singing to the ebullient music, and even when she talks in clichés, the words seem newly minted. It's somehow clear that the "fun" she's talking about isn't just superficial fooling around, it's the real thing; she's talking about reaching her creative potential, finding herself, "walking in the sun." And it's contagious—somehow we just know that her parents will soon be out there in the sun with her.

"Girls" is so contagious that it's caught on all over

the world. In Japan it has been retitled, for some inscrutable reason, "New York Danceteria." Japanese teenagers, it would appear, enjoy reading English words regardless of whether they make any sense. For example, emblazoned across a sweatshirt recently "smuggled" in from Japan are the following words:

50's ECCENTRIC BOY
HIGH-HEELED
SUPER ROCK 'N' ROLL FEELING COSTUME

This may mean something in Japan, but it doesn't make a lot of sense where English is spoken. Ah, well. "Girls Just Want to Have Fun" may make no sense in Japanese.

Incidentally, as soon as Cyndi made "Girls" a hit, advertisers around the world began to approach Robert Hazard for permission to modify the song for use in their advertising campaigns. Don't be surprised if you hear a jinglized version of it coming out of your radio one of these days. (For more on "Girls," see chapter 8.)

"WHEN YOU WERE MINE" by PRINCE. Starting with its crackling drum-synth riffs and its roller-rink–carnival-sounding synthesizer melody line, "When You Were Mine" has a real circus atmosphere about it. The obvious question that a first-time listener has is "What's going on here?" Is this, like those old Doris Day and Patti Page tunes, supposed to be heard as a man's song being sung by a woman? Or is Cyndi twisting that concept here, doing what was originally a man's song as a woman's song? Since this is Cyndi Lauper, we pretty much have to assume that the latter is the case and that what we're hearing in the lyrics is the description of a very modern relationship. In other words, we assume we're not supposed to pretend to be listening to a man telling a woman that he knows she's going with another guy but that we're actually hearing a woman telling a man that she knows *he's* going with another guy. This is the 1980s, after all.

And so we're thrown into the middle of a day in the life of two (or three) people with a somewhat edgy lifestyle. They all seem to have trouble making decisions—the woman singing can't bring herself to get mad when she discovers her boyfriend's boyfriend sleeping between them (a scene you'd never have found in a Patti Page song or even a Ronettes song); the boyfriend obviously can't make up his mind about anything (other than that he likes to wear her clothes); and who knows what the boyfriend's boyfriend is thinking.

It's a real mess.

At the end of the second verse, Cyndi hits an impossible note and we realize that the singer's persona is both crazy and tenacious—the mixed-up boyfriend is probably never going to shake her no matter how many new boys he drags into her bed. And, of course, circulating through the entire piece is the ultimate plaint of the spurned love junkie: "I love you more than I did when you were mine." At one point, near the end, Cyndi's voice actually sounds like the voice of a crying baby, which is perfectly consistent with the character she's playing in this bent scenario.

And then once or twice near the end (around the time the guitar starts twanging in a style reminiscent of Duane Eddy's), she changes the plaint to what sounds like "I loved you more when you were mine," contradicting everything that went before. Oh well, that's par for the course with this sort of relationship.

"TIME AFTER TIME" by CYNDI LAUPER AND ROB HYMAN. Culture critic David Blum considers "Time after Time" to be the most universally do-able song on the album, meaning that he can as easily imagine it being sung by Frank Sinatra or Tony Bennett as by Cyndi. It is also, he says, "her closest shot at Muzak—it'll be heard in elevators and dentists' offices for years to come."

Perhaps the reason for this is that, musically, "Time after Time" manages to be simple and haunting at the same time; it's a song with a melody that is easy to hum and impossible to forget. Couple this with Cyndi's singing and a clean arrangement featuring a bass drum "heartbeat" and a wistful, phase-shifted guitar, and the song is an instant classic.

What about the lyrics? Well, there are those who feel that the whole is less than the sum of the parts—the lyrics are a mite too impressionistic to add up to an easily comprehensible story line. Some listeners have claimed that the song is about time travel, but they're in a distinct minority. Since when was an easily comprehensible story line important in a rock 'n' roll song, anyway? (See chapter 9 for more on "Time after Time.")

SIDE TWO:

"SHE BOP" by CINDY LAUPER, S. LUNT, G. CORBETT, AND RICK CHERTOFF. Cyndi's "h—hey" is at its peak in "She Bop," and there's no way properly to punctuate her little "oop" that comes before the "she bop" at the end of each verse. Cyndi explains that the song came about one day when she and some of her collaborators happened to be looking over a copy of *Blueboy* magazine. They got to talking about how no one's ever written a song about *that* subject, and before they knew it, they were working on what might be the first-ever rock paean to masturbation. Is Cyndi's convent training showing in the tongue-in-cheek line in which she hopes "He" will understand?

In addition to its scandalous subject, "She Bop" has a number of other notable features. It's the first song ever to conjugate the verb "to bop." It redefines both the direction south (as in "I wanna go south 'n' get me some more") and the phrase "danger zone" (as in "I can't stop messin' with the danger zone"). Further high points are Cyndi's heavy-breathing solo during the instrumental break and her giggles—some of the cutest in the history of rock 'n' roll—which are sprinkled throughout the song.

Other than that, the synthesizer-whistler duet that precedes Cyndi's breathing is just plain nifty. What more can you ask for from three minutes and forty-three seconds?

Note: The "She Bop" video is being completed as this book goes to press.

"ALL THROUGH THE NIGHT" by JULES SHEAR. Jules Shear, an EMI recording artist whose "When Love Surges" video clip received a fair amount of play on MTV, wrote this tender ballad. From the opening bar, with its synthesizer arpeggios, its sound evokes an earlier generation of wistful rock ballads such as the Safaris' "Image of a Girl" or the Cascades' "Rhythm of the Rain."

Lyrically, "All through the Night," in its obsession with moving forward and reaching back in time and its impressionistic imagery, seems to be related to "Time after Time." It also seems, with its line "until it ends there is no end," to be related to Yogi Berra, the baseball great who coined the phrase "It ain't over till it's over."

As with "Time after Time," many people who adore "All through the Night" haven't the faintest idea what it's all about, even if they spend hours every day singing it to themselves. You are invited to analyze it yourself in twenty-five words or less. Hint: It's definitely *not* about time travel.

"WITNESS" by CINDY LAUPER AND JOHN TURI. This is the one song on *She's So Unusual* that Cyndi cowrote with her songwriting partner from Blue Angel. The song's highlights include Cyndi's slightly raspy, resigned yet energetic vocals, the percussion and keyboard instrumental, and the cheerleader background vocals. You can definitely dance to it!

"I'LL KISS YOU" by CYNDI LAUPER AND JULES SHEAR. This song can be viewed as the long-awaited sequel to the Clovers' 1959 hit "Love Potion Number Nine." What's funny about it is that despite the two-and-a-half decades that have passed since the

Clovers recorded their song, the protagonist of "I'll Kiss You" still hasn't figured out how to use a love potion.

The singer of "Love Potion Number Nine," you may recall, visited the gypsy (Madame Ruth was her name) because he was a "flop with chicks." He glugged down the potion on the spot, then "started kissing everything in sight." The tale ended when he kissed a cop, who broke his bottle of potion and presumably had him locked up overnight on a drunk and disorderly charge.

The mistake the poor fool made was that he fed the potion to the wrong person. As everyone knows, you *never* drink a bottle of love potion yourself. The idea of it is to make someone else—preferably the object of your affection—drink it so that *they* fall in love with *you*. Drink it yourself, and you might find yourself in big trouble!

Alas, the protagonist of Cyndi's "I'll Kiss You" still doesn't get it, even after the unpleasant experience she says she had with love potion number eight. Instead of slipping it into her boyfriend's cherry Coke, she gets into a taxi and drinks the bottle herself. As expected, she experiences the usual symptoms, then ends up on the corner (of Thirty-fourth and Vine, no doubt), where everyone looks great to her. Despite her optimism, there's a fairly good chance that things aren't going to work out the way she wants them to—her boyfriend's not there yet, the hour's getting late, she's seeing double . . .

One further note: "I'll Kiss You," in addition to being seen as a sequel, may also be seen as an homage by Cyndi and Jules Shear to the great songwriting duo of Jerry Lieber and Mike Stoller. In addition to writing "Love Potion Number Nine," Lieber and Stoller co-wrote "Hound Dog" and wrote "Treat Me Nice," "Jailhouse Rock," and "Loving You" for Elvis Presley, "Ruby Baby" and "Drip Drop" for the Drifters, "Black Denim Trousers" for the Cheers, "Stand by Me" for Ben E. King, "Young Blood," "Poison Ivy," "I'm a

CYNDI

LAURIE PALADINO

LAUPER

AL MAURO

EBET ROBERTS

*P*revious page: Cyndi Lauper, finally having fun.

*A*bove: Rick Derringer jams with Blue Angel at Studio 54.

*N*eilson, Morelli, Lauper, and Brovitz of Blue Angel.

EBET ROBERTS

AL MAURO

LAURIE PALADINO

*Y*esterday and today: Cyndi in Blue Angel (top left), and on the set of the "Girls Just Want to Have Fun" video.

LAURIE PALADINO

EBET ROBERTS

Cyndi giving it her all, time after time.

AL MAURO

*F*ormer tag team partners Cyndia Lauper and "Captain" Lou Albano.

LAURIE PALADINO

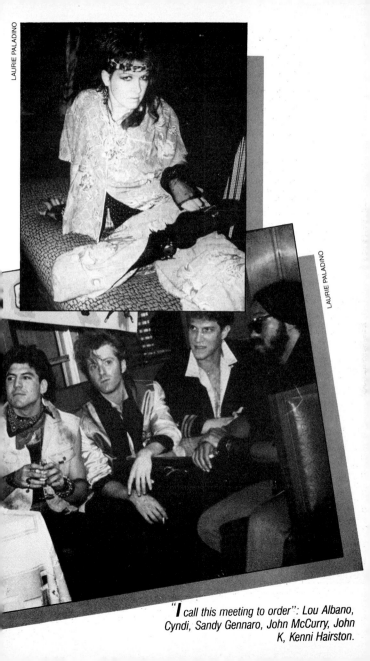

LAURIE PALADINO

LAURIE PALADINO

"*I* call this meeting to order": Lou Albano, Cyndi, Sandy Gennaro, John McCurry, John K, Kenni Hairston.

*C*yndi and Rodney Dangerfield try to get some respect.

LAURIE PALADINO

LAURIE PALADINO

LAURIE PALADINO

*S*hades of Cyndi.

Cyndi and John McCurry onstage.

Bottom right: Cyndi plays lead uke on "He's So Unusual."

LAURIE PALADINO

EBET ROBERTS

LAURIE PALADINO

LAURIE PALADINO

*Y*ipes, stripes.

*C*yndi and the band flash Hollywood smiles.

*A*bove right: All trussed and nowhere to go.

EBET ROBERTS

*T*hey came from outer space: Cyndi and
Dave Wolff in the ''She Bop'' video.

Hog for You," "Charlie Brown," and "Yackety Yak" for the Coasters, "I'm a Woman" for Peggy Lee, "Kansas City" for Wilbert Harrison, and dozens of other classics from the fifties and sixties.

"HE'S SO UNUSUAL" by AL LEWIS, AL SHERMAN, AND ABNER SILVER. A hoary classic from 1929, the heyday of Tin Pan Alley, it might be about the guy the protagonist of "I'll Kiss You" is waiting for on the corner.

Out of the right speaker comes the thin, scratchy sound of an old seventy-eight: It's Cyndi's incredible imitation of Helen Kane (the real-life singer who was the inspiration behind Betty Boop), accompanied by an acoustic piano. She gets through the first verse when suddenly the whiplash of a synthesizer blasting into both ears launches us a half century ahead, right into "YEAH YEAH," by M. RICKFORS AND H. HUSS, and we're thankful to be living in the age of rock 'n' roll.

This song, the last one on the album, is a flat-out rocker distinguished by telegraphic lyrics that could have been distilled from countless rock classics, a fine Eric Bazilian sax solo, and Cyndi's little Betty Boop (who somehow has managed to stick around) voice in the background saying things like "Oh, Ignatz, I loves you" and "I want sushi. . . ." And every time the "yeah, yeah" refrain comes around, Cyndi's little character seems to be holding onto the reins—she's not used to this rock 'n' roll stuff here in the future. This is the true time-travel song on the album, and it's a great one.

Speaking of "He's So Unusual," you may be wondering if the album's title came from the title of the song. Cyndi says it did but only indirectly. One day, after a recording session, Cyndi, Rick Chertoff, and some of the other musicians and studio personnel were relaxing in the studio. Chertoff, talking to a friend on the phone, happened to say that he thought Cyndi was wonderful. Cyndi laughed and said that's what they ought to call the album: *Cyndi Lauper—She's Wonderful*. The engineer, familiar with the song "He's So Unusual," immediately said, "No—*She's So Unusual*." It stuck.

Listening to the album, it's clear that Cyndi wasn't choking on other people's songs the way she had done in her cover-band days; she was finally able to mold her material, to sing every song as if it were her own. Of Jules Shear's "All through the Night," for example, Cyndi says, "I used a harshness to portray a harsher side of life that I actually lived. And what I pulled from it really upset me. I had a difficult time, but I knew that it was right because it was in my heart."

Of course, great material and great vocals do not necessarily add up to a great album—the musicianship has to measure up as well. There's no question that on *She's So Unusual* it does. In addition to Rob Hyman and Eric Bazilian on guitar and keyboards, Rick Chertoff enlisted a stellar cast of studio players to back them up: Anton Fig on drums, Neil Jason on bass, Richard Termini on synthesizers, Rick DiFonzo on guitar, Peter Wood on synthesizer, William Wittman on guitar, and Rick Chertoff himself on "extra percussion." The backup singers are top-notch as well. It's clear from the number of rock's top talents who worked on *She's So Unusual* that Cyndi has finally been recognized by her peers as well as by the rock 'n' roll public as one of the most significant new artists recording today.

Just for the record, backup singer Ellie Greenwich is herself a songwriting great. With her partner Jeff Barry and producer Phil Spector, she cowrote such girl-group classics as "Da Doo Ron Ron" and "Then He Kissed Me" for the Crystals, "Be My Baby" and "Baby I Love You" for the Ronettes, "Chapel of Love" for the Dixie Cups, and many, many more. She also cowrote, with Cyndi and J. Kent, "Right Track Wrong Train," the song that appears on the flip side of the "Girls Just Want to Have Fun" forty-five. Listen to it and see if it doesn't remind you of the Shangri-Las doing "Leader of the Pack," which Greenwich cowrote in the mid-sixties. Cyndi, quick to praise a collaborator, says of Greenwich, "She's such a craftsman, and she was so great to work with once I got over being in awe of her."

Cyndi wanted to control the look as well as the sound of her first solo album; with her background in the arts, she was qualified to do just that. The front side, a photograph of Cyndi frozen in time in front of a stylized, run-down New York building with the late baseball star Roberto Clemente's name over the door and posters for "the wax musée" hanging on the graffiti-covered facade, looks like a painting—which was exactly the effect Cyndi was going for. The picture on the back contains an even more overt and certainly more surreal art reference. In the background, slightly out of focus, is the Coney Island Parachute Jump; in the foreground are Cyndi's legs, yellow bobby socks and white shoes. On the soles of her shoes, amazingly, are details from *Starry Night* by her favorite painter, Vincent van Gogh. Both photos were taken by famed photographer Annie Liebowitz.

She's So Unusual was released officially on October 14, 1983. Unlike *Blue Angel*, an album that entered— and exited—the market in relative obscurity, *She's So Unusual* had the critics talking right from the beginning.

The *Los Angeles Times* raved. "She warbles, she hiccups, she squeaks and squeals and sounds like a giddy cross between Betty Boop and Melanie.... Lauper's sure-handed control and intelligence turn one of rock's most unusual voices into a powerful, thoroughly charming instrument. Throw in her excellent taste in material and you have a record that bounces with zesty abandon.... Best of all is her own 'Time after Time,' in which she downplays her mannerisms and lights up the luminous, quietly resolute love song with an aching, heartfelt vocal. It's the knockout punch on one of the year's most delightful surprises."

Cash Box, the record industry's venerable trade weekly, said, "With the hiccuping delivery of an ultra-hip Betty Boop, a flaming multi-hued mane and a wardrobe that would be the envy of any Eastern European gypsy camp, Lauper is not your run-of-the-mill spandex and Danskin rock vocalist. But beneath the chic Lower East Side styling beats the heart of a true rocker, and the proof is on her album."

Leslie Bermans, in the *Village Voice*, reviewing Cyndi from a feminist point of view, said, ". . . as women's issues get muddied under differences of class, style, aspiration, and sexual preference, polarizing and diluting the heroines and ideals I once championed, I'm glad to find a strong, sexy, funny, smart female role model to point out, I hope, to my own daughter someday. I think Emma Goldman [the famous anarchist writer and spokesperson], for one, would have liked to have her in the revolution."

In what must surely rank as one of the most interesting record reviews of all time (you can decide for yourself whether it's a positive or a negative review), Greil Marcus writing in *Art Forum* (that's right—*Art Forum!*)—and using language such as ". . . high and low voices signify different emotional languages, and it's the clear transition from one to the other that signifies the signifiers, that allows them to communicate"—concludes that Cyndi Lauper's true vocation is to disturb people, to wake them up. Of Cyndi's version of "Money Changes Everything," he says, "Whether or not money changes everything, it's patent that singing this song changed Lauper, if only into more of a singer—which is to say that a confrontation with questions of value intensified her will to ignore the rational transitions of song-texts, to the point that the radio may be unable to transmit that will without suffering damage in the process. And that is finally to say—as, driving around town, I twist the dial in search of another Lauper media shock—that she can wake people up because she can herself be wakened." Whew!

And finally, *Rolling Stone*, the Bible of rock 'n' roll, was unabashedly upbeat about *She's So Unusual*, affectionately describing Cyndi as "the finest female junk-rock vocalist since the heyday of the great Maureen Gray, more than twenty years ago." The review continues, "Like Gray... Lauper has a wild and wonderful skyrocket of a voice—the epitome of pre-Beatles girl-group pop—and at her best, as she often is on this smartly produced solo debut, she sounds like a missing musical link with that long-gone golden age.... when Lauper's extraordinary pipes connect with the right material, the results sound like the beginning of a whole new golden age."

Golden age indeed! It finally looked like Cyndi's career was on the right track.

CYNDI ON INSPIRATION

"I was always inspired by other artists, growing up hearing these voices in my head that followed me around constantly, which always gave me purpose and inspiration and courage...."

CYNDI TAKES
OFF

*A*lthough the critics were virtually unanimous in praising her album, Cyndi's solo career did not take off instantaneously. In fact, on December 29, 1983, over two months after *She's So Unusual* was released, Cyndi found herself opening for the antediluvian Kinks at New York's famed Roseland Ballroom. When she came onstage her reception was no more hospitable than that granted most other openers: She was rudely greeted with the cheer "We want the Kinks! We want the Kinks!" Cyndi didn't let the crowd get to her, though—she blasted through their indifference with a pyrotechnic display of both vocal technique and stage gymnastics. According to one critic, she was like "A young Lucille Ball on speed. She danced with the band, vaulted onto the speakers, and generally covered the stage the way volcanic lava covers unwary cities."

By the time she arrived at the surefire grabber "Girls Just Want to Have Fun" (which only a handful of people in the audience had heard before), most of those Kinks fans were hanging onto Cyndi's every gesture. Her magic had won them over.

In April of 1984, Cyndi played another large New York room, the Ritz. This time, though, things were different: Cyndi was the top attraction, and she sold out the house for three nights running! What had changed in the four months since the Roseland show?

One word: Television.

Between December and April, the music video of "Girls Just Want to Have Fun" had gone right to the top of MTV's playlist, was picked up by the other music video shows on cable and network TV, and blasted Cyndi to national prominence. To complement her music video exposure, Cyndi had made the rounds of such network television programs as "The Tonight Show," "Late Night with David Letterman," "The New Show," and the Grammy awards ceremony (not to mention a number of appearances on TV wrestling programs along with her "mentor" or "adviser," "Captain" Lou Albano; more on *that* later). In these appearances, she and her new touring band usually performed (live and un–lip-synced) "Girls Just Want to Have Fun" and "Time after Time" to the delight of the live studio audiences and the folks at home—not only was Cyndi's material superb and her singing spectacular, but the way she *looked* . . . wow! Record stores and radio stations from coast to coast were suddenly hearing a new cheer in the air: "We want Cyndi Lauper! We want Cyndi Lauper!"

What was most amazing about Cyndi on TV wasn't her singing, though—her fans always knew she could sing—but the fact that during the interviews, she handled herself like a trouper. On "The Tonight Show," for example, she was one of the best first-time guests to ever grace Johnny Carson's hotseat—she had Johnny in stitches with her Betty Boop voice, her uncanny comic timing, and her wacky perspective.

She started out—after doing "Girls Just Want to Have Fun"—saying that if she weren't singing, she'd probably be a brain surgeon or a rocket scientist. Then, without blinking, she segued into a hilarious routine about how Johnny ought to manipulate "The Tonight Show" backdrop—Wizard of Oz style—to match the stories his guests told. For sad stories, she said, Johnny could make it rain, for happy stories he could bring out the sun, for long, rambling stories he could go through the seasons at will, and so on. Old friends and fans of Cyndi's may have known that she was just applying her highly evolved visual sensibilities—in a comically twisted way, of course—to the show's familiar set. To the people in the studio audience, though, it was straight humor, and they guffawed in appreciation. So did Ed McMahon and the evening's other guest, comedian Robert Klein. (Klein later said he feels that Cyndi has it in her to be a great comedienne: "Her timing is superb.")

No sooner had the people in the studio stopped laughing than Cyndi launched into an explanation of the P.E.G. principle and how it applied to her and others in show biz. P.E.G., she said, stands for Politeness, Etiquette, and Grooming. She ascribed the concept of P.E.G. to her "personal manager," Captain Lou Albano, who has at various points in his career actually managed a stable of bad-guy professional wrestlers with names like the Wild Samoans, Mr. Fuji, and the Magnificent Morocco. With Gracie Allen–like logic, she asserted that politeness was basic to both rock 'n' roll and wrestling. She then explained that etiquette is especially important to show-biz types because in a business where so many deals are made over lunch or dinner it is imperative to know how to eat without spilling food all over the table. Then on to grooming, which, according to Cyndi, is "everything" to both rockers and wrestlers. As paradigms of good grooming, she cited herself and the Wild Samoans.

After Cyndi performed "Time after Time," Johnny Carson invited her to come be a guest on the show again, to which she replied, "Yeah, it's a very famous thing to do, I guess." She then demonstrated something she called "the Hollywood smile," got a final laugh from Johnny and the audience, and the show was over.

It was a terrific performance, a true star performance. And we're not even talking about her singing!

It didn't hit Cyndi that she was a star, a real star,

until the day she arrived at NBC's New York studios, located at Rockefeller Center, to be interviewed on *Live at Five*, a local talk show. Seeing a few people waiting around outside the studios, Cyndi assumed that some big act was appearing on *Late Night with David Letterman*, which is taped in the same building. To her surprise, the fans were there for *her* autograph. After the show there were even more people waiting for her. "Oh, there's my public, awaiting me," she joked, but the fans were perfectly serious—they wanted Cyndi! As she signed a bunch of autographs, she realized that this was it, that it had really happened: She'd made it!

It's a little strange, when you think about it, that Cyndi Lauper, who'd spent nine years working in bands, taking voice lessons, and perfecting her singing skills needed to become a television star before becoming the rock 'n' roll star she always knew she could be. Oh, well—it was true, and neither Cyndi nor anyone else was complaining about it.

After *She's So Unusual* hit the market in October of 1983 and before Cyndi's television appearances had brought her fame, she and Dave Wolff realized that they couldn't just sit around and pray that people bought the album—the time had come to take the Cyndi show on the road, which meant the time had come to put together a working band, a real road band for touring and promotion. The musicians who had played on the album all had other studio commitments or, as in the case of Rob Hyman and Eric Bazilian, groups of their own, so putting a band together meant starting from scratch.

Putting a band together was a more complex project than it would have been some years earlier. There was more at stake now than ever before and potentially many more people watching. Since this was to be Cyndi's band and since Cyndi's style is unique both musically and visually, the musicians had to be chosen with special care. "In looking for musicians," Dave

Wolff told an interviewer, "everything was equal. I wanted a total package: ability, the look—including a willingness to change the look, to be somewhat chameleonlike but still not lose their own identity—and a good, professional attitude."

The idea from the start was to build a band, not to buy one. Wolff says they were looking for people who were not only good musicians but whose personalities and styles would mesh with Cyndi's. Through referrals from other good musicians and music-business professionals, Cyndi and Dave selected a group of potential band members to interview. "I interviewed about twenty-five people," Wolff says, "and found about ten that might work. Then I had everyone meet individually with Cyndi so that they would have a sense of who everyone was before being thrown together in an audition. We nursed it along, rather than coldly throwing it together." He adds, "Cyndi is extremely dynamic, sometimes unusual and contrary to the norms. I wanted people who could complement that. And if you take the time to do it right, it'll work."

Four musicians made it through this screening process to the final cut: John McCurry on guitar, Kenni Hairston on keyboards, Sandy Gennaro on drums, and John K on bass.

Guitarist JOHN McCURRY has a shock of red hair that almost matches Cyndi's psychedelic hues. Onstage, it's John who lends Cyndi a shoulder to cry on during the tearjerker finale of "Time after Time."

John hails from Connecticut, where he taught and played guitar before moving to New York City. He lived in New York for two years, working with other musicians on demo tapes, recording jingles for commercials, and doing some work with David Bowie's guitarist, Carlos Alomar, who introduced John to Wolff and Cyndi. Their first meeting was not unlike a standard job interview in that John didn't audition—it was assumed that he could play or he wouldn't have been recommended—but rather he discussed his music and his goals. Needless to say, he passed with flying colors.

John's first task was to learn the album. This wasn't particularly difficult for a guitarist of his caliber because the album contains a lot more synthesizer work than it does guitar parts; in fact there isn't one major guitar solo on the record. (Listen to it and see for yourself.) As he and the band started working together, however, John began to find places where he could insert a tasty guitar lick or two without changing the character of the song or the arrangement. Cyndi sees her band members as equals, so she encouraged John and the others to explore the tunes they would soon be performing in front of audiences. By the time the band was ready to hit the road, the show contained three of John's solos, and he continues finding new ways to introduce his guitar sound into Cyndi's songs.

With his long dreadlocks and trademark sunglasses, synth-wiz KENNI HAIRSTON looks like he arrived in New York directly from the Caribbean. Don't be deceived by his looks, though—Kenni is actually a native of Virginia, USA. Onstage he provides the complex and sometimes lush synthesizer backdrops to Cyndi's performance. Because *She's So Unusual* is so much a synth-based album, Kenni probably had the toughest time of all the musicians learning his parts. This didn't bother him, though—he's a seasoned keyboard player and picked right up on Cyndi's style.

Kenni, who has no qualms about admitting he came to the Big Apple for "money and success," had played in a number of regional bands before making his big career move to New York. (Before hooking up with Cyndi, he had backed up the likes of James Mtume, the Ritchie Family, and Nona Hendryx; each of these experiences expanded his skills and brought him closer to attaining his personal goals.) Like John McCurry, he met Dave Wolff about two years after arriving in New York, flew through the job interview, and found himself in a hot new band. He refers to Cyndi as "a redheaded ball of excitement." It would be hard to find anyone who disagreed.

With his black leather clothing and his tattoos, SANDY GENNARO is the quintessential rock 'n' roll drummer from Staten Island. With his credits—he played with Pat Travers, Benny Mardones, Blackjack, and Carmine Appice—he was a shoe-in for the band. In fact, he almost played on the *She's So Unusual* sessions, but a previous touring commitment made that impossible.

Although Sandy didn't mind that the plan for the band was to stick pretty closely to the arrangements and sound of the album, he was concerned at first that he would have to rein himself in. Sandy, you see, is a very intense drummer. Fortunately, Cyndi isn't the type to hold back an intense drummer—she told Sandy to knock himself out. Watching him play, you can see that that's exactly what he does, and he loves every minute of it.

"I think the magic of this band," Sandy told *International Musician and Recording World* magazine, "is that we're all from different backgrounds, and the mixture and the chemistry present something completely different from those backgrounds."

The band member with the shortest last name is bassist JOHN K. John has had an unusual career, having played both with David Bowie and the late Klaus Nomi, the conceptual-artist-cum-rock 'n' roller who, though largely unknown in North America, achieved a fair measure of success in Europe.

John met Bowie through Carlos Alomar, the same person through whom John McCurry met Dave Wolff. One night, according to K, Alomar said, "I got some work for you. I'll tell you about it later." The work, which he very nonchalantly mentioned later, turned out to be playing bass behind David Bowie on "The Tonight Show!"

John K wasn't sure at first if Cyndi's band was going

to work out because everyone seemed to be coming from a different musical background. Obviously, he needn't have worried about it—the arrangement has worked out just fine.

Of Cyndi, John K says, "She's such a complete artist. She has all the elements that I would say make up a great artist; someone who can go beyond the one hit. She can write, she can sing, and she is consistently visual."

And Cyndi's as happy with her band as they are with her. In fact, in a number of promotional situations where the star traditionally goes it alone, she has insisted that the band accompany her. And on television, where many stars would be content to lip-sync, Cyndi not only brings the group with her so they can play live, she makes sure that each band member gets a fair share of time on camera as well.

"I'm a feel singer and a band person," Cyndi sums up, "and I have so much fun with these guys."

And where did Cyndi and her new band play? Take a look at this hectic schedule from a one-month period in the spring of '84:

April 7	Framingham College, Framingham, Mass.
April 8	Toad's Place, New Haven, Conn.
April 11	Temple University, Philadelphia, Pa.
April 12	Metro, Boston, Mass.
April 13	Agora, Hartford, Conn.
April 15	University of Bridgeport, Bridgeport, Conn.
April 18	Brandywine, Chad's Ford, Pa.
April 19, 20, 21	The Ritz, New York City
April 24	Park West, Chicago, Ill.
April 25	Agora, Cleveland, Ohio
April 26	Grand Circus, Detroit, Mi.
April 29	State University, Buffalo, N.Y.
May 3	University of Maryland

May 5	Rumors, Atlanta, Ga.
May 6	London Victory Club, Tampa, Fla.
May 7	Button South, Miami, Fla.
May 9	River Boat, New Orleans, La.

Not a bad month for a new band! And don't forget they were about to take off for a trip overseas, to such widely separated countries as Germany, Australia, and Japan, where Cyndi played to some of the most enthusiastic audiences she'd ever faced.

SHOP TALK

The shape of a musician's guitar pick, the size of a drumstick, the model number of a synthesizer— these details are of little interest to the average fan. However, to other musicians or to superfans they're crucial information. Herewith, the equipment you would handle if you won the opportunity to be Roadie for a Day in Cyndi's traveling band:

Drummer Sandy Gennaro pounds on a Ludwig kit equipped with Paiste cymbals, plus a Simmons snare and toms. His sticks are five-eights.

John McCurry plays a traditional Fender Stratocaster customized with a Floyd Rose tremolo setup and a humbucking pickup in the bridge position. In addition, he keeps a Gibson ESP around as a backup. When he's going for a dirty sound, he plays through a Marshall fifty-watt amp; for clean sounds he uses a Roland. He gets his special effects through two MXR digital delay boxes and an Ibanez harmonizer.

John K plays through either a nifty new Steinberger bass or a vintage 1963 Fender

Precision. He plugs them into Ampeg SVT amps.

Kenni Hairston plays a Roland Juno 60, an Oberheim OBX-A, and a Yamaha DX-9 through a delay unit and a chorus.

———————————

The reviews of Cyndi and the band's live performances were generally as enthusiastic as the reviews of *She's So Unusual* had been a few months earlier.

Critic Laura Foti, after seeing Cyndi at the Ritz, said, "Lauper and other characters from her video clip 'Girls Just Want to Have Fun' cavorted onstage in a re-enactment that underscored the video's strength of concept and Lauper's star qualities. . . . The rest of Lauper's performance was a nonstop series of spasmodic theatrics and breathtaking vocals. . . . Lauper is the real thing, a brilliant and honest performer with more than a touch of eccentricity and a thousand volts of electricity. . . . At the end of an hour the audience was exhausted but Lauper was still onstage—or dancing through the audience—seemingly unaware that collapse could ever be a possibility."

David Frankel, in *New York* magazine, had this to say: "Live . . . Cyndi is every bit as kinetic and alluring as her video: She devours the whole stage, sashaying with her old-fashioned skirts and petticoats, dancing loose and free or tight and furious, playing coy or vampish, throwing in sudden bits of friendliness . . . Through it all there's her humor, which taps a great pop tradition of smart silliness. In doing so, Lauper touches rather tenderly on some of the enthusiasms many listeners felt for rock 'n' roll on first hearing it."

The *New York Times* characterized Cyndi as ". . . a singer with considerable drive and theatricality and a flamboyantly exotic appeal." However, in a rather downbeat ending, the reviewer complained that while Cyndi's music was "solidly delivered," it was not particularly original. Oh well, can't win 'em all.

In a press release dated April 13, 1984, at the height of her East Coast tour, Portrait Records made an announcement that must have been music to Cyndi's ears. It began with the bold headline "CYNDI LAUPER AND SINGLE STRIKE GOLD; New Video and Single Released as Headline Tour Commences." It continued,

All the world loves a Lauper—CYNDI LAUPER, that is! Her debut Portrait album *She's So Unusual* and its first single "Girls Just Want to Have Fun" have both been certified Gold, for sales over 500,000. . . . As CYNDI LAUPER'S train of fame keeps a-rollin', she's found new fans among black record buyers. They're turning the Arthur Baker extended remix of "Girls Just Want to Have Fun" into the hottest 12-inch disc on the market. And the poignant ballad "Time after Time" has just been released as Cyndi's second single, accompanied by a new video already receiving heavy airplay on cable music outlets like MTV. . . .

The train of fame was a-rolling, all right. Her records, her live performances, her television appearances, and her videos—especially her videos—were all working together to make Cyndi the hottest new female vocalist around.

GIRLS JUST WANT TO HAVE FUN

Captain Lou Albano, a 313-pound retired TV wrestler turned wrestling manager, is being interviewed on a wrestling program. He has biceps the size of most people's thighs, long curly hair, a scraggly beard that on this occasion is held in place by a rubber band, an earring, and a Hawaiian shirt the size of a lean-to wrapped around his bearlike bulk. Astonishingly, he is taking full credit for Cyndi Lauper's success, claiming that he made her what she is today and that without him Cyndi would be back where she belongs—in the kitchen getting pregnant! He speaks, or growls, so quickly it's impossible to keep up with him.

Suddenly Cyndi, sporting her new striped hairdo, wearing the usual array of jewelry and brightly colored clothes, appears from backstage and approaches the captain. He instantly starts yelling at her. Cyndi is calm at first, but Albano finally gets to her. Exasperated, Cyndi starts yelling back. When this fails, she starts smacking him with her pocketbook. The captain yells something that sounds like "You're a disgrace to your family, to yourself, to your mother"—here he pretends to spit—"to your grandmother, to everyone involved. . . . *I* wrote the music, *I* wrote the lyrics, *I* directed the video, I took you from a barroom broad and made you a lady. Got it, Lauper? Made you a lady. . . . if that's possible! . . ."

In another broadcast Cyndi, addressing Albano as "fatso," insists that he knows even less about wrestling than he knows about music and challenges him to a match between his best woman wrestler and a woman wrestler Cyndi says she herself will manage. "Oh, you're gonna get hurt," is about the only comprehensible response Albano makes.

Later in the broadcast, a reticent Dave Wolff is brought onstage. The live audience, a wrestling rather than a rock 'n' roll crowd, is somewhat surprised to hear that Captain Lou isn't Cyndi's real manager and gives Wolff a halfhearted show of applause. In response to the announcer's request to clear up the controversy, Wolff explains that the only thing Albano had to do with Cyndi's success, in addition to introducing her to the P.E.G. principle, was to play Cyndi's father in the "Girls Just Want to Have Fun" video, no more no less. Did Albano produce, write, or direct the video, the announcer asks? Of course not, Wolff says, claiming that the captain has fabricated the rest of it as a publicity stunt, and a very offensive one at that. He goes on to say that Albano actually had the nerve to approach Portrait Records and demand money for having made Cyndi what she is today. As Albano starts shouting at him from the wings, Dave calmly explains a new principle to complement the P.E.G. principle. He calls it the B.A.D. principle, for Beaten, Annihilated, and Destroyed, which is what's going to happen to Albano's female wrestler when she and Cyndi's wrestler meet in the ring. Albano, practically foaming at the mouth, screaming incomprehensibly, charges Wolff, threatening to destroy him, Cyndi, and their female wrestler all at the same time.

What is going on here?

Let's backtrack a bit. Cyndi says she met Lou Albano on an airplane trip to Puerto Rico a few years back while she was still with Blue Angel. Impressed by his earrings, the rubber band in his beard, and his sheer magnitude, she asked him for his autograph and

suggested that maybe they could work together some-
time: Cyndi thought it might be fun to do a humorous
record commercial. The captain gave Cyndi his phone
number and that was the last they saw of each other
for a long time.

Dave Wolff, it turned out, had been a TV wrestling
fan for years. When he and Cyndi got together, she
started watching it, too. Week after week she saw her
old buddy, Captain Lou, mouthing off on TV. (The
captain, in case you haven't figured it out yet, is a
notorious loudmouth famous for screaming at announ-
cers, referees, and his wrestler's opponents.)

Albano, in the meantime, was already involved to
some extent in the music business as the nominal manager of yock-rock band NRBQ. And so it seemed natural, sort of, when Cyndi called him up to see if he'd
like to act in her first video, "Girls Just Want to Have
Fun." He wasn't sure at first, but at the last minute,
he said he'd do it. (He also makes a cameo appearance
as a waiter in "Time after Time.")

Albano was then officially christened Cyndi's personal adviser, or mentor, which evidently means that
it was his job to teach her his now-famous P.E.G.
principle. What else it means is shrouded in mystery.
One thing is clear, though: Regardless of what he says,
the captain was never Cyndi's actual business manager; insinuate that he was when you're within earshot
of Dave Wolff, and you're liable to find yourself the
victim of a flying knee drop or a figure-four leglock!

As to what went wrong with Cyndi's and the captain's relationship, that, too, is shrouded in mystery.
One day they were friends—Cyndi quoting Albano on
network television and appearing with him on wrestling
shows—and the next day Albano was insulting her and
Dave on TV. Only one thing is certain: Despite the
orchestrated look of this conflict, it is *not* just a hoax
or a publicity stunt. Lawyers for both sides reportedly
are preparing to battle it out in the forensic arena just
as Cyndi's and Albano's wrestlers are preparing to tear

each other apart on the wrestling mat. The outcome of the next round is as unpredictable as the previous rounds have been preposterous.

Cyndi, who wishes the whole ridiculous situation had never come about, sadly sums up what she now thinks of Captain Lou Albano: "The guy's a slug."

In any case, the "Girls Just Want to Have Fun" video introduced both Cyndi and Captain Lou to a whole new audience, the viewers of MTV. Music television, though only two years old when "Girls" was released, was already well on its way to becoming a vital force in the music business and the entertainment industry as a whole.

CYNDI ON VIDEO

"Video should portray a new side of the artist to the listener, who can now see this person they've been listening to and feel their persona and understand more about them and know them better. I think that video is as important as the record, because it's who you are."

MTV didn't invent the idea of making films to accompany records. For years many European jukeboxes have been equipped with small rear-projection screens that show a film to go along with the selection playing on the box. Even in the United States and the United Kingdom there have been many short films made over the years to promote individual rock 'n' roll songs. The perennial problem with these films, of course, was that there was nowhere to show them except on the occasional rock TV show or (as in the case of the Blue Angel films) at film festivals and other places where film, or rock, cognoscenti gather. Consequently, the films had very little promotional value, which means that record companies were hesitant to spend money on them. Generally, only those recording artists who were commercially successful and who had strong backgrounds in the visual arts as well—David Bowie comes to mind—really got to work in the medium.

What MTV did was provide a place where these short films could play all day and all night long, the visual equivalent of rock radio. This meant that there was an instant demand for rock video clips. Suddenly, instead of being the exclusive domain of a handful of artists, the medium of film, or video, was open to all groups and individual performers with promotional-minded record companies behind them.

And the record companies were quick to catch on. They were looking for a new way to promote their artists. Ever since the music explosion of the late sixties, record sales had been weak. Even disco, in the mid-seventies, hadn't brought the industry back to its former sales levels. The blame was variously placed on the aging of the baby boom generation, on the weak economy, and on changing taste patterns. Whatever the cause, the record industry was unhappy about the results. The advent of MTV and its imitators, though, held the promise of a new way to reach music fans and revive their appetite for new records.

An average music video clip, including "Girls Just Want to Have Fun" and "Time after Time," costs in the neighborhood of twenty thousand to forty thousand dollars to produce. (An exceptionally elaborate video—Michael Jackson's "Thriller," for example—might cost a *lot* more, but that's a whole other story.) This is only about a third the cost of an average thirty-second TV commercial, but record companies were originally unwilling to spend even that much money on any but their hottest groups. This is because videos were seen as a luxury or, in some cases, a concession to an artist who insisted on trying out the new medium. Soon, though, it became clear that the groups making videos were beginning to sell more records than those who weren't making videos. Record execs, whose livelihood depends on their ability to pick up on trends, realized that video was no longer a luxury but a necessary promotional tool that happened to be an especially effective way to introduce new acts to a large audience. As video took off, newcomers like Duran Duran, Culture Club, Men at Work, the Eurythmics—and Cyndi Lauper—started skyrocketing to superstardom as fans who had discovered them on video flocked to buy their records and concert tickets.

How does a video get on MTV in the first place?

First, record companies send MTV (which is a division of the giant Warner-Amex entertainment conglomerate) their video clips on three-quarter-inch video cassettes. (Occasionally, a band that has self-produced a video will send in a half-inch cassette, the size used by home video machines.) All new tapes—and there are twenty to thirty of them that arrive every week—are screened by a ten-person acquisition committee. The first test is whether or not a clip is technically up to snuff. If the picture and the sound measure up to broadcast standards, the video is then transferred to one-inch tape. At this point, the tech people at MTV can make adjustments in the clip: Static can be filtered out, the color can be improved, the sound can be enhanced (often by rerecording from the original masters), and so on. This is also when the credits are "Chironed" (a computer titling process) onto the clip. After all this is done, the final version is transferred again, this time to a two-inch cassette.

After a video has been okayed for play on MTV, the next question is *how often* it will be played. Most video clips—including "Girls Just Want to Have Fun"—start out in what's called "light rotation." This means the video is shown once or twice every twenty-four hours. If a clip proves to be popular after a few weeks, it may move up to "medium rotation," which means it gets played three times a day, or "heavy rotation," which means it gets played four times a day. Of course, if a group has already established its popularity on MTV, it may start right out on a "medium" or "heavy" rotation (as did "Time after Time"). MTV isn't sent directly to your TV set from MTV headquarters, by the way—it's first beamed to a satellite, then back down to your local cable operator for distribution.

How does MTV know what viewers want to see? Simple—they do a phone survey of about three thousand viewers every week. ("Girls Just Want to Have Fun" was a huge hit with MTV viewers in the telephone surveys.) Of course, the people at MTV also watch the record charts. If a record is in the Top Ten, its video is bound to get heavy airplay on MTV.

How do you go about making a music video? First you need a recording artist with some hot tunes. If the artist is particularly colorful, if the material lends itself to visual representation, or if the artist has a good visual sense, so much the better. Then you need a record company willing to pay for the production, plus a director and a producer to actually get the clip made.

Cyndi Lauper obviously qualifies as an artist with good material. She also is an undeniably colorful performer with a visual-arts background plus a strong sense of what it is she wants to say with her music and her videos. As Dan Beck, a merchandising director of Portrait Records, told the *Wall Street Journal* in what might have been the understatement of late 1983, "Cyndi was signed because she'll be a great film performer; she has the dynamics to create interesting visuals." Portrait's game plan was for "Girls Just Want to Have Fun" to be both the first single and the first video clip from *She's So Unusual*.

So with her record company picking up the tab, Cyndi started working with director Ed Griles (the same

Ed Griles who directed the Blue Angel videos) and
producer Ken Walz (whose previous production was
at the opposite end of the spectrum: a commercial for
Wonder Bread!). Then all they needed was a crew of
twelve or fifteen hardworking movie production people, a zany cast of actors, and choreography to match.

Yes, choreography. Cyndi wanted there to be dancing in "Girls" because she feels that dance, like music,
is good for the soul. However, as she didn't want clas-
sical, Broadway, or TV type dancing, she couldn't work
with just any choreographer. Her choice was new wave
dance group XXY.

This is how XXY was described in a pamphlet for
the Tompkins Square Festival (in New York's East
Village), dated September 18, 1983:

> XXY Dance/Music is a collective founded by Cyndi
> Lee and Mary Ellen Strom with composer Pierce
> Turner. Since 1981 the company has committed it-
> self to the exploration of social and political con-
> cerns and to the investigation of structural forms
> mutually shared by music and dance, in both cases
> applying the tools of contemporary technology to
> deepen artistic and public awareness. The work of
> XXY has been presented by such organizations as
> the Whitney Museum, Dance Theater Workshop,
> Brooklyn Association of Arts and Culture, Dance
> on the Lower East Side at Dancespace, St. Marks
> Church, and the Riverside 10-Cents-A-Dance Roof-
> top Festival. Pierce Turner is a member of the Major
> Thinkers . . . who have performed with XXY at the
> Savoy and the Ritz.

The Major Thinkers, you'll remember, are also managed by David Wolff.

Cyndi insists that "Girls" is no ordinary video, where
the performer is presented with a scenario and told
what to do by a director; it is an artist's video, not a

video with an artist in it. "If the artist doesn't have much to do with their video," Cyndi says, "that's like making a record that you don't have much to do with. In that case, you don't need the artist—you can just use anyone." Not only was the video's overall concept Cyndi's, but many of the details were hers as well.

For example, in a radical break with moviemaking tradition, she arrived early at Mothers Sound Stages, where all the interior scenes were shot, to help decorate the set. (Mothers, incidentally, was chosen not only for its large studios, its convenient location, and its reasonable rental fees, but for its luxurious double-size "star" dressing room. Cyndi was thinking "big time" even before her album was released!) Most of the props you see in the video—postcards, pillows, posters, an old record player, old forty-fives—really do belong to Cyndi. She personally painted the furniture, à la Jackson Pollock: She spread newspapers on the floor of the studio, got hold of a brush and a can of paint, and splattered away until she was satisfied. She was even involved in the wardrobe, having final approval over what the other actors were wearing.

The interiors were shot on Sunday, September 11, 1983. (The set had been prepared that Friday and Saturday.) Because of the limited budget, the crew was small and the shoot was hectic—everyone was running around doing two or three jobs at once. Nevertheless, once they got rolling they didn't stop, and the shoot was completed more or less on schedule, which is atypical in the often disorganized low-budget world of music videos.

One of the reasons things went so well is that Cyndi had done her homework and, along with director Griles, knew exactly how she wanted everything shot. In fact, Cyndi was so concerned about making every shot perfect that she practically codirected the clip, nervously hopping from one detail to the next, fixing a prop, commenting on the lighting, directing an actor. Griles had to keep telling her to relax, but she didn't take her eye off the set until the time came for her to go to her dressing room and put on her makeup.

One of the actors Cyndi most enjoyed coaching—and of whom she was proudest—was her mother. ("Isn't she great?" Cyndi would say every time her mother finished a take.) She also was happy to be working with her brother, Butch, who is in the crowd scene, and her old friend, folk-rocker Steve Forbert. They'd worked together before—Blue Angel had opened for him a few years back. Just for the record, he's the shy boyfriend fighting his way through the crowd to deliver a bouquet of flowers to Cyndi toward the end of the clip. (In July of '84 Steve played the Lone Star Café in New York. Just for fun, Cyndi—unannounced—got up on stage to sing with him. So did Huey Lewis of the very hot band Huey Lewis and the News. Now *that* would have made a great video!)

Another friend Cyndi was glad to be working with was Lou Albano, who cuts a real swath through the video playing Cyndi's father and looking something like a retired Hell's Angel. "I'm an equal opportunity employer," Cyndi laughs.

When it came time to shoot the final scene in the bedroom, Cyndi decided she wanted the room *filled* with people, far more people than were on the set at the time. Cyndi describes her vision of the scene: "The door opens and a roomful of people fall out . . . like in 'A Night at the Opera.'" Furthermore, the people who were to fall out had to be a little *strange* looking. If the clip had been shot anyplace else, this might have presented major casting, makeup, and wardrobe problems. Luckily, Mothers is located on Fifth Street at Cooper Union, a mere three blocks from Saint Marks Place, New York's new wave Main Street. Once the talent coordinator put out the word, appropriately attired young men and women started flooding into the studio. It was Ken Walz who finally suggested that it was time to lock the doors and get on with the show.

The exterior scenes of "Girls Just Want to Have Fun" were shot all over lower Manhattan, including Greenwich Village and the Wall Street area. At one point, when they were shooting near the corner of Gay and Christopher Streets in the Village, Cyndi complained to Ed Griles that some of the extras were too *normal*-looking. She then proceeded to grab some of the more *interesting*-looking pedestrians who were passing by (and there are always plenty of them in that part of town) and press them into the service of "Art."

After two hectic days, Griles had shot a total of over two hours of exteriors (shot at twenty or more locations) and interiors for the four minutes of the video. This was then cut to the length—and to the beat—of the song by editor Pamela Wise.

In editing, the "Girls Just Want to Have Fun" clip includes an advanced special effect that was never before used in a music video. Griles and Walz wanted a visual equivalent for the joyous instrumental section of "Girls." They decided that since it has such a "bubbly" feel to it, they would try to create a bubbly look for that part of the video.

At Broadway Video, a state-of-the-art video post-production house in New York, they found a way to add computer-designed bubbles to the clip. (Both "Girls Just Want to Have Fun" and "Time after Time" videos were originally shot on film. This is because starting out with film gives the finished product a better look than starting out on videotape. Tape, though, is easier to edit; many video makers transfer the film footage to tape for editing and special effects.) Broadway Video had only recently acquired a new piece of editing equipment called a Quantel Mirage computer. The Mirage, which can do just about anything with a visual image, had been used for commercials and TV title sequences, but it had never before been used in a music video.

Walz and Griles didn't let this deter them. They took original images from the video—pictures of Cyndi and

friends—and had the Mirage "wrap" these images into
the shape of bubbles for the instrumental sequence.
For the background, they had the machine create plain
bubbles. The experiment was clearly a success: The
bubbly instrumental sequence is one of the most entertaining parts of a thoroughly entertaining video.

When it was finished, Cyndi was very happy with
the clip. So were the viewers of MTV—they liked it
so much it was tracked into heavy rotation not long
after it arrived on the play list. The video's success
went on to help make the single of "Girls Just Want
to Have Fun" and the entire *She's So Unusual* album
a smash, the album selling over one million copies by
the summer of 1984. "I was really hoping the song
would be a hit," she told an interviewer, "and it is.
And the thing that's so touching about it to me is that
I really put my best foot forward. I sang my best and
tried to do something that was real. That kind of sin-
cerity goes across to the people. They aren't stupid.
They know when it's real."

Doing "Girls Just Want to Have Fun" was also a
good way for Cyndi to say something positive about
women. Explaining that she's a feminist ("And that
doesn't mean a wild woman from Borneo who hates
everyone"), she says that listening to the lyrics while
you watch the video will make it clear that the song is
a subtle feminist statement. Her favorite line in the
song, she says, is "I want to be the one to walk in the
sun"; she loves overhearing young girls walking down
the street singing the line. She also loves the story the
song tells: the daughter coming home late, the parents
starting to give it to her, and then the daughter turning
around and liberating her mother, her father, *and* herself. It's an especially interesting story line when you
remember that Cyndi's real-life mom appears in the
clip.

As to why the single of "Girls Just Want to Have
Fun" didn't take off until the video started getting no-
ticed on MTV, Cyndi has a theory: "Maybe it's be-

cause if you just hear it, this weird girl voice, you don't understand what I'm trying to say. Maybe it took the video to capture it."

Whatever it took, it worked.

TIME AFTER
TIME

*A*nyone who has watched an hour or two of MTV knows that the majority of music video clips consist of performers either in a concert setup (a stage, microphones, ecstatic fans, and so forth) or in a modified concert setup (a stage-type performance in an unusual setting, such as in bed, on a beach, in a hot tub, or on a set dressed to look like Stonehenge after World War III). Either way, the artists are doing essentially what they do in front of a live audience except that they are lip-syncing rather than actually playing.

While this approach does produce some interesting results, more often than not it provides little more than a linear visual gloss to accompany the song. Cyndi's approach to video, on the other hand, is to tell a visual story that complements the song. Because she feels that video is as important a medium as records, she puts as much artistic energy into conceiving and "composing" a video clip as she puts into her music.

The lyrics of "Time after Time," for example, are about leaving, waiting, falling behind, and catching up. There is nothing in the lyrics that suggests what kind of world is being pictured in the singer's suitcase of memories or why the singer is walking ahead in the first place. Depending on your point of view, the video provides either a concrete and highly detailed subtext for the sketchy, abstract lyrics or an entirely separate

but related story told in visual counterpoint to the story
line of the lyrics.

Without going into elaborate detail, the story told
in the video is about a young woman living in a very
small town who one day decides it's time to expand
her horizons. She announces this decision by symbol-
ically changing the way she looks. Her small-town boyfriend doesn't approve of the change—he's not ready
to move ahead with her. But she knows what she wants
and needs; she has to go whether or not he comes with
her. After saying good-bye to her mother, who, it would
appear, has spent her life sweeping small-town floors,
and trying one last time to get her boyfriend to change
his mind, the young woman leaves town. The final
sequence is poignant—she's not breaking up with him,
just doing what she has to do; it's clear that he can
come along as soon as he's ready.

The video is obviously a lot more complex than it
had to be—Cyndi might have been content to simply
sing the song as she sat in a bedroom or wandered
along a beach, but that's not her style. What makes it
worth the effort is that "Time after Time" is as beautiful
and unforgettable a video clip as it is a song.

A number of people were interviewed about "Time
after Time" recently in a little experiment designed to
determine just how memorable Cyndi's second video
really is. Although none of the people had seen the clip
more than a few times, they were asked to describe it
step-by-step. A woman in her early twenties gave the
following account, which is typical of those given by
the others interviewed:

"The first time you see her, Cyndi Lauper, she has
normal honey-blond hair. She's with her boyfriend, or
manager, or whoever he is. In the second scene they're
in a funky-looking diner—it all takes place in the suburbs, by the way. There are already some other people
sitting in a booth with her boyfriend. She comes in
wearing a big hat. She takes off her hat, and her boyfriend sees she's changed her hair—now it's a new-

wave sort of orange. He doesn't like her hair. You get
the idea they're having a fight about it. She runs out
of the diner, and he runs down the street after her.
Where the song talks about going forward and falling
behind, she hides in a doorway and he runs past her.
She escapes, but she's not happy about it. Then she
goes to visit her mom, who's busy sweeping up. Next
time we see her, she wakes up in this little trailer. It's
sort of in the woods—you get the idea she lives there
with him. She packs her stuff in a plaid bag and leaves.
He wakes up and sees her leaving. He runs after her
and takes her to the train station . . . or maybe they go
to her mom's first so she can say good-bye. Then they
go to one of those little suburban train stations. In the
station he tells her he's not going with her to wherever
she's going. (I assume she's going to the city, some-
place she'll fit in with hair like that!) She's upset that
he won't come, but the train's there already, so she
gets on by herself. She looks out the window of the
train. It's one of those separation scenes like in the
old movies—he's standing there getting smaller and
smaller as she looks out the window. She's crying. The
end."

Despite a few inaccuracies, the description is amazingly detailed, especially considering that our inter-
viewee hadn't seen the clip for a while. The other
interviewees all had equally vivid memories of "Time
after Time," even those who didn't consider themselves hard-core fans.

Cyndi must be doing something right.

Regardless of what a film or video finally looks like,
film sets—even on comedies—are often rather grim
places to work, at least for the actors. For long stretches
of time the only people doing anything are the camera
people or the lighting people or the set people or the
props people or the director working with all of them
at once; the actors are usually the last ones to do their
thing, even though they have to be ready to jump into

their roles at a moment's notice. This means that even when they're hanging around in their trailers waiting to shoot a scene, they can't fully relax—they don't know when they'll be given the call to get back into character.

There were a couple of reasons why being on the set of "Time after Time" was more difficult for Cyndi than being on the set of "Girls" had been. For one thing, there was more riding on "Time" than there had been on "Girls." Cyndi wasn't a star while "Girls" was being made; if it had failed completely—for example, if it had been so awful that it didn't get on MTV—only a handful of people would have known or cared. Because "Girls" had been a hit, however, there were a lot of people—fans, execs in the music business, television and movie people—waiting to see how "Time after Time" would turn out. In other words, there was a pressure to excel.

In addition to this pressure to excel, there was the usual pressure that any actress feels while waiting to go on camera, plus the added pressure that Cyndi always puts on herself no matter what she's doing. Because she's a perfectionist about her work, Cyndi tends to be very serious on the set and in the studio.

Also, the subject and mood of "Time after Time" is darker, heavier than the good-time "Girls Just Want to Have Fun." (Cyndi calls "Time after Time" "a real tearjerker.") This may have influenced Cyndi's mood throughout the three-day shoot, making her more aware of all the little things that could go wrong.

And finally, because the shoot went slowly almost from the beginning, Cyndi was concerned that the whole project was going to fall impossibly behind schedule.

Why did the shooting go slowly? For one thing, it was late in the winter of 1984. In New Jersey, where the video was shot, it was bitterly cold and windy, making it very difficult to get around and nearly impossible to shoot outdoors. For another thing, in the months that had passed since September, when "Girls" was shot, Cyndi had become a bona fide star. This meant that every time she and the crew set up for an outdoor shot, a crowd of bundled-up fans would suddenly materialize, making filming even more difficult.

The first scene in any film is not necessarily the first scene the director shoots. There are any number of reasons for this. Perhaps an actor or a location is only available on a certain day. Or maybe the first scene requires snow, and it happens to be the middle of summer. Or there are two locations side by side, and it's convenient to shoot them sequentially even though they don't appear sequentially in the finished movie. Because there are so many variables, it is a rare film indeed that is shot entirely in sequence.

Music videos, like any other kind of film, are often shot out of sequence. The first scene shot for "Time after Time" was actually the final scene in the finished video clip—the scene with Cyndi on the departing train. And the second scene shot happened to be the second-to-last scene in the video, the sad scene inside the train station where Cyndi and her boyfriend (played, of course, by David Wolff) have their final tête-à-tête. Interestingly, although the finished clip gives the impression that both scenes were shot at the same train station, they were actually shot at two different stations—one of the stations was better for the interior sequence, the other was better for the exterior shots.

Strange as it seems, the normally outgoing Cyndi was shy about performing the emotional "breaking up" scenes in the train station and the final sequence on the train. During the shooting, she requested that the set be cleared of everyone but the director and essential camera people. Any other crew members who had to remain on the set but who weren't specifically required to be watching the action were told to turn their backs on the actors. It wasn't that Cyndi had trouble crying for the camera—as the finished video shows, she was very convincing. She just didn't want to do it in front of the entire crew. (Yes, those are real tears.) These

were difficult shots to film, and it took several takes
to get them right. By the time this part of the shoot
was finished, many of the people working on "Time
after Time" were close to exhaustion.

On the second day of shooting, a local radio station
put out the word that Cyndi Lauper was shooting a
video in Wharton, New Jersey. This may have been a
real service to her fans, but it didn't help Cyndi at all.
By the time she and the crew arrived at the first location of the day, which was the little trailer, there was
a crowd of between three thousand and four thousand
fans waiting to greet them. The local police were also
out in force, putting up barricades in an effort to keep
the fans from swarming all over Cyndi, the crew, and
the set.

Cyndi's mother, who by now had adopted the stage
name Catrine Dominique, was scheduled to act in a
scene that morning and had traveled to the location in
the same bus as Cyndi. When the bus arrived at the
location and she saw the enormous number of fans
waiting for Cyndi, Catrine started to cry—the reali-
zation that her daughter was really a star, with thousands of fans willing to come to a small town in New
Jersey just to see her shoot a video clip, was too much
for her. Then Cyndi started to cry, and pretty soon the
entire back of the bus was filled with people crying.
For Cyndi, it was reminiscent of the fans asking for
her autograph outside the NBC studios, only this time
on a much grander scale. And, of course, there was
the added bonus of being able to share the experience
with her mom—who seemed to be even more deeply
moved by it than Cyndi was.

The next location planned for that morning was a
house located a scant two minutes' walk from the trailer.
Since it was an exterior shot, the last thing Ed Griles
and the crew needed was a few thousand fans yelling
and screaming while they were trying to get their shots.
As a ploy, members of the crew drove Cyndi all around
town in circles as fans tried to follow them on foot and

in other cars. It was like a scene out of a wild-goose-chase movie, except that Cyndi was not particularly amused—the chase was taking up precious time and threatening to break her concentration and everyone else's. All they wanted to do was to get back to work.

Finally, when it seemed they had lost their followers, the crew members drove Cyndi to the house location as Griles and his staff set up for the scene. Needless to say, within an hour the entire crowd had discovered and virtually surrounded the new location.

The "Time after Time" video was originally scheduled for a two-day shoot, but when the end of the second day arrived there were still scenes that hadn't been shot. While it's no big news for a film to go slightly over schedule, it can be a much bigger problem for a music video production than for a commercial, TV, or movie production. There are two reasons for this. First, as the shoots are short, a single extra day can be a substantial percentage of the total shoot. Second, because the budgets are usually low, there just isn't a lot of room for error or for extra days. (On a big-budget feature film set, a single day's shoot can easily cost twenty thousand or thirty thousand dollars. Even with the scaled-down standards of music videos, a day's shoot costs a substantial chunk of money.)

Fortunately, the remaining scenes were mostly interiors, which are much easier to control than are exteriors—a thousand eager fans can't just wander into an interior set as easily as they can surround an exterior location. When it was time to pack up at the end of the third day, there was nothing left to shoot.

"Time after Time" was "in the can" and ready to be edited.

INTO THE
FUTURE

CYNDI ON CYNDI

"I'm happy. I'm doing what I want in life. For years I thought I was really a failure, and I'm not—I can sing."

*B*y the time this book is in your hands, Cyndi's third video, "She Bop," will have been released, her second solo album (and probably her fourth video clip) will be in production, the outcome of the wrestling match between Cyndi's and Lou Albano's female wrestlers will have been decided, and an ever-growing, worldwide audience of fans will be waiting eagerly to find out what Cyndi's next move will be.

Cyndi's talents lie in so many directions that it makes little sense to try to make precise predictions. Of course she'll continue to write songs, to make records and videos, to do concert tours and appear on TV, and of course, like any serious artist, she'll continue to grow both personally and professionally. The real question is *what else will she do*?

As an example of what she might do, it was recently announced that Cyndi plans to design her own line of clothing. Now, this could sound ridiculous coming from any number of other entertainers, but from Cyndi the announcement is believable. She does, after all, have a strong visual-arts background, and there's no doubt that she's put together her own wardrobe with exceptional panache. Why shouldn't she put together other people's wardrobes as well?

Those with an ear to the ground have reported rumors that Cyndi's planning to write a book and that she's being considered for a starring role in a major Hollywood movie. (She visited with the Muppets recently, and *Rolling Stone* ran a picture of her with Rizzo the Rat. Some fans immediately assumed she was planning an appearance in the next Muppets movie.) At one point there was a rumor abroad that she was going to be a regular on a weekly network television comedy program or that she was being considered for her own show. It matters little whether these rumors turn out to be well founded; the point is people are beginning to relate to Cyndi Lauper as the kind of person who can do just about anything she sets her mind to, and this gives credibility to even the most outlandish rumors.

Are predictions about Cyndi's personal life in order? As visible as she is professionally, Cyndi prefers to keep a very low profile personally. She's a hardworking artist, not the type of entertainer who hires a press agent to talk about her love life. She has said, however, that while she's very happy with Dave Wolff, she has no plans to marry him or anyone else. This doesn't mean she's not interested in children: "I'd like to have children," Cyndi says, "and I'd like to have a family, but not in the traditional structure and the traditional sense."

Of course, with a new star there's always reason to wonder: Is this a passing fad or is it the real thing? With Cyndi there's every indication that it's the real thing. Above all, there's her voice. Even if she stopped writing songs, wore drab clothes, dyed her hair a mousy brown, and lost her sense of humor, she'd still have that magnificent voice. Add everything else she has going for her—her many other talents, her belief in herself, her perfectionism, her drive—and it's hard to imagine that she won't be around for a long, long time.

And so, rather than our ending the book with a solemn series of predictions that will in all likelihood appear hopelessly dated in a year or two, *you* are going to make the predictions yourself by checking yes or no to each of the predictions on the list that follows.

First, though, write down today's date so that a year from today you can score yourself according to the directions at the end of the prediction list.

Today's date is _____

INSTRUCTIONS: Check either the Yes or the No box preceding each of the predictions. Some of the predictions are serious, some are silly, but all of them count in your final tally. Don't forget to make up predictions of your own at the end. One year from today (well, it's all right if you're off by a day or two), score your predictions to see how many of them have come true.

YES   NO

[ ]   [ ]   **1.** Cyndi becomes America's leading export.

[ ]   [ ]   **2.** Cyndi and Michael Jackson record a song together.

[ ]   [ ]   **3.** Cyndi's second album goes double platinum.

[ ]   [ ]   **4.** Cyndi publishes her autobiography.

[ ]   [ ]   **5.** Cyndi is on the cover of *People*, *News-week*, *Vogue*, and *Creem* magazines at the same time.

[ ]   [ ]   **6.** Cyndi wins her first Grammy.

[ ]   [ ]   **7.** Cyndi stars in a major motion picture.

[ ]   [ ]   **8.** Lou Albano and Cyndi star in a new TV series based on *The Honeymoon-ers*.

[ ]   [ ]   **9.** Cyndi and her band travel to Japan. They're met at the airport by thousands of screaming fans wearing Cyndi wigs.

[ ]   [ ]   **10.** Cyndi and Paul McCartney record a song together.

[ ]   [ ]   **11.** Sparkle gets top billing in a made-for-TV movie.

[ ]   [ ]   **12.** Cyndi wins her first Oscar.

[ ]   [ ]   **13.** Cyndi retires from singing to devote her full attention to managing a stable of professional wrestlers.

[ ]   [ ]   **14.** Cyndi founds a new musical movement: permanent wave.

[ ]   [ ]   **15.** Cyndi and Boy George record a song together.

[ ]   [ ]   **16.** Cyndi publishes a cookbook.

[ ]   [ ]   **17.** Cyndi becomes a brain surgeon *and* a rocket scientist; wins her first Nobel Prize.

[ ]   [ ]   **18.** The Gallup poll reveals that over 99 percent of all Americans now can pronounce Lauper correctly.

[ ]   [ ]   **19.** Sparkle wins an Emmy.

[ ]   [ ]   **20.** Menudo makes Cyndi an offer she can't refuse; she says she'll join the group on the condition that it change its name to "Menudo featuring Cyndi Lauper."

[ ]   [ ]   **21.** Cyndi publishes an autobiographical cookbook.

[ ] [ ] **22.** One of Cyndi's tag teams wins the world championship.

[ ] [ ] **23.** Lou Albano and Cyndi star in a new TV series based on *The Twilight Zone*.

[ ] [ ] **24.** Cyndi introduces her own line of designer clothing.

[ ] [ ] **25.** Cyndi introduces a line of "Girls Just Want to Have Fun" dolls and "Time after Time" watches.

[ ] [ ] **26.** Cyndi is on the cover of *Soldier of Fortune* magazine.

[ ] [ ] **27.** Lou Albano appears on the cover of *G.Q.*

[ ] [ ] **28.** Late one night, when the moon is bright and the sky is clear, Lou Albano actually is inspired to write a song. It is recorded by Weird Al Yankovic.

[ ] [ ] **29.** Cyndi starts a band with Michael Jackson, Paul McCartney, and Boy George.

[ ] [ ] **30.** Cyndi introduces her own line of designer hair.

[ ] [ ] **31.** Sparkle introduces a line of designer leashes, tags, and flea collars.

[ ] [ ] **32.** Cyndi sells out three consecutive nights at Madison Square Garden.

[ ] [ ] **33.** Cyndi becomes the first woman president of the USA; "Girls Just Want to Have Fun" is declared the national anthem.

[ ] [ ] **34.** Your prediction: _____
_____

[ ] [ ] **35.** Your prediction: _____
_____

HOW TO SCORE: One year from now, go over your predictions to see how many you were right about. Keep track of your score here:

Number right: _____   Number wrong: _____

WHAT YOUR SCORE MEANS:

If you scored

Over 30 right	You're either a true Cyndi Lauper fan or one of the world's leading psychics
25–30 right	You're hip, cool, and with it
20–25 right	You're hip and cool
15–20 right	You're hip
10–15 right	You're there
5–10 right	Are you there?
Under 5 right	Have you ever considered becoming a professional wrestler?

APPENDIXES

DISCOGRAPHY

She's So Unusual (Portrait CBS)

Side One
Money Changes Everything
Girls Just Want to Have Fun
When You Were Mine
Time after Time

Side Two
She Bop
All through the Night
Witness
I'll Kiss You
He's So Unusual
Yeah Yeah

Singles (Portrait)

Girls Just Want to Have Fun b/w Right Track
Wrong Train
Time after Time b/w I'll Kiss You
She Bop b/w Witness
Girls Just Want to Have Fun twelve-inch dance
single
I Had a Love
Fade
She Bop twelve-inch dance single

With Blue Angel:
Blue Angel (Polydor)

Side One
Maybe He'll Know
Anna Blue
Can't Blame Me
Late

Side Two
Cut Out
Take a Chance
Just the Other Day
I'm Gonna Be Strong
Lorraine
Everybody's Got an Angel

Single (Polydor)

I Had a Love b/w Take a Chance

VIDEOGRAPHY

From *She's So Unusual*:
Girls Just Want to Have Fun
Time after Time
She Bop

CYNDI LAUPER INTERNATIONAL FAN CLUB INFORMATION

Contact CYNDI LAUPER FAN CLUB
c/o Sixty-Five West Entertainment Co., Inc.
65 West Fifty-fifth Street, Suite 4G
New York, New York 10019